MANAGING, MARKETING, and BUDGETING for the A/E OFFICE

MANAGING, MARKETING, and BUDGETING for the A/E OFFICE

George O. Head, Jr.
Jan Doster Head

VNR VAN NOSTRAND REINHOLD COMPANY
New York

Library of Congress Catalog Card Number 88-24
ISBN 0-442-20493-0

Printed in the United States of America
Designed by Azuretec Graphics

Van Nostrand Reinhold Company Inc.
115 Fifth Avenue
New York, New York 10003

Van Nostrand Reinhold Company Limited
Molly Millars Lane
Wokingham, Berkshire RG11 2PY, England

Van Nostrand Reinhold
480 La Trobe Street
Melbourne, Victoria 3000, Australia

Macmillan of Canada
Division of Canada Publishing Corporation
164 Commander Boulevard
Agincourt, Ontario, M1S 3C7, Canada

16 15 14 13 12 11 10 9 8 7 6 5 4 3 2 1

Library of Congress Cataloging in Publication Data

Head, George O., 1945–
Managing, marketing, and budgeting for the A/E office / George O. Head, Jr., Jan Doster Head.
p. cm.
Includes index.
ISBN 0-442-20493-0
1. Architectural firms—United States—Management.
2. Architectural services marketing—United States.
3. Architectural firms—United States—Finance 4. Engineering firms—United States—Management. 5. Engineering services marketing—United States. 6. Engineering firms—United States—
—Finance. I. Head, Jan Doster. II. Title.
NA1996.H43 1988
720′.68—dc19 88-24
CIP

CONTENTS

PART 1: A/E MANAGEMENT / 1

Introduction / 3
Phase Task Codes / 4
Time Accounting / 15
Utilization Rates / 26
General Ledger / 29
Overhead Rate / 36
Bidding (Project Cost Estimating) / 40
Job Costing / 45
Client Billing / 50
Accounts Payable / 58
Work in Progress / 61
Payroll / 63
Conclusion / 74

PART 2: HOW TO MARKET A/E SERVICES / 77

Introduction / 79
Is This You? / 81
What Is Marketing? / 89
Who Is the Client? / 96
Building the Data Base / 104
Intelligence / 118
Advertising / 125
Public Relations / 135
Selling / 143
Referrals / 161
Conclusion / 165

PART 3: COST MANAGEMENT / 167

Introduction / 169
The Cost Analysis Survey / 171
Types of Costs / 178
Funny Money / 186
Cash Management / 191
Payroll Costs / 196
Budgeting / 203
Hidden Costs / 208
Internal Controls / 214
Conclusion / 221

Glossary / 223
Index / 229

PART 1
A/E MANAGEMENT

Introduction

The purpose of this part is to assist individuals with the responsibility of business and project management of architectural/engineering and design firms. Although the concepts presented here represent sound business management theory that is applicable to a broad range of businesses and industries, the main focus is the A/E firm.

Anyone who has worked in one already knows that this type of organization has some very unique problems and challenges in organizing proper business and project management controls in order to compete effectively in today's market. Although professional architects or engineers may wish to apply their disciplines without regard to the bottom line, it is a hard fact of life that a firm must make a profit in order to stay in business. Budgeting, project management, time accounting, estimating, contract negotiation, and a myriad of other management skills must be learned and applied if the firm is to survive and grow.

The concepts presented here are not the result of economic theory, but of actual experience in working and consulting with literally hundreds of firms since 1981. We have had the opportunity to test the concepts taught here in the real world, and we know they work. We are confident that they can help any A/E firm that will consistently apply them.

What follows is designed to work with either an automated computer system or a manual system. Naturally, the size of the firm will dictate the efficiency of using a computer system over a manual operation. It is our firm belief that a computer cannot do the thinking for you. Its purpose is to take the drudgery out of day-to-day operations and to give you in minutes what may take days to produce manually. But you must understand the reasons for the things you do before you can use a computer efficiently.

Phase Task Codes

Phase task codes are probably the single most important concept in proper time and project management. As you will see, the proper use of phase task codes becomes the cornerstone of any organizational system.

What is a phase task code? The term is familiar to many and totally foreign to others. Any activity during a given day has a purpose. If someone were to ask you what you are doing you might say:

"I'm working on this drawing."
"I'm filling out my time sheet."
"I'm attending a staff meeting."
"I'm meeting with a client."
"I'm reading this book."
"I'm taking the day off."
"I'm eating cake at the office birthday party."
"I'm just sitting here."

Needless to say, if you own or manage the firm, you might consider some of these activities a little more important than others and might express some degree of satisfaction or dissatisfaction over the responses. Obviously some of the above activities will be more productive and make more money than others. And at the same time some activities, even though they do not directly make money, may be equally important.

What is important is to be able to account for not only how much time employees and owners are spending on tasks but also what they are doing with the time.

There have been many books written on proper time management theories, and it is not our purpose here to teach you how to get the most out of the time available to you. What we want to teach you is how to account for the time you spend and to apply a cost to that time in order to know, before you lose money, the results of spending time on different activities.

We have seen company after company bid out projects on a flat fee or hourly basis without the slightest notion of what their costs for doing that project will be. Many times their first indication that there might be a problem is when they have to see their banker. The work is there. Their employees are all busy. They are losing money. And they do not know it.

THE PHASE

The phase task code is divided into two parts. As the name implies, the phase is one part and the task is the second. Architects are extremely familiar with the term *phase.* Familiarity, however, does not necessarily mean understanding. The AIA has divided the work that an architect does into phases, as follows:

Predesign services
Site development
Design development
Schematic design
Bidding and negotiation
Construction documents
Contract administration
Additional services

This list serves as a good starting point in the definition of a phase. But do not be confused if the above terms are not familiar to you, and do not confuse the job performed in these phases with the purpose of the phase itself.

The above phases are used by architects to define the scope of services that they perform for clients. The list indicates a loose chronological order for the performance of these services. This chronology is not necessary for our purpose. What is important is that these phases represent broad activities for which specific tasks are performed. The fact that they may have another purpose, such as the orderly performance of a project, is so much the better.

If someone were to ask you what you can do during any given day, the list might be somewhat long. Depending upon your creativity, you may be able to come up with several hundred items or several thousand. Therefore you must have a way of properly grouping given activities so that they represent some organization, or they simply become meaningless.

The phase is the highest level in the organizational hierarchy of activities. As such its use should be kept to a minimum. Phases should be broad, general categories representing the major activities that your firm performs. In addition to the above phases, which are typical of architectural offices, the following is a list of possible phases that could be used by engineers and design firms:

Surveying
Mechanical engineering services
Electrical design
Interior design
Furniture procurement
Layouts
Structural engineering services
Water analysis
Title work
Modeling
Specifications
Accounting
Time off
Programming
Marketing

Needless to say, the phases that any given company defines are unlimited. The phases for a company must be meaningful and useful for that company. Although many firms have several things in common as to the scope and type of projects they do, each firm has some phases that are unique to that individual company.

Although the phase is generally the broadest category in time organization, there is one other division of time that is even broader and of equal importance. That is indirect and direct time. Phases are naturally classified as direct, those generally applicable to particular projects, and indirect, those mainly applicable to general administrative duties. Accounting, general marketing, and time off are all examples of indirect phases, as they do not directly relate to specific projects. This division of time will be discussed in more detail in its own section.

Naturally no one project will include all the phases available to a firm, but the proper identification and implementation of phases will aid in the analysis of an ongoing project and will give vital information on methods of salvaging a potentially sour project. You will then have the ability to recognize a problem early rather than constantly performing postmortems on projects.

THE TASK

The phase is a broad grouping of the general activities performed by each firm. The task, on the other hand, is a more detailed itemization of these activities. Some examples of tasks may be:

Project administration
Client conferences
Drafting
Completion of time sheets
Schematic design
Interior design
Survey taking
Compiling management reports
Errand running
Blueline printing
Word processing
Presentations
Model construction

One of the important things to note is that you can never perform a phase. You can only perform tasks. Many times, however, a task within a major phase might have the same description as the phase. For example, schematic design may be a phase; you of course can perform many different tasks, such as client conferences, preliminary drawings, and presentations, as part of that phase. You can also prepare schematic designs as a task in the schematic design phase.

Another important thing to remember is that the phase and the task should be considered as a unit, not as a group of phases and a group of tasks which can be combined in any unlimited manner. As an example client conferences may be a task in several phases; on the other hand it is uncommon to do a survey in the interior design phase. Therefore each phase should have only certain tasks that are authorized for it. This unit is called the phase task code.

The number of phase task codes will differ from organization to organization. Some companies can very effectively manage their operations with as few as 40 or 50 phase task codes, while others need 200 to 300. There is no exact, optimal number. Generally speaking single-discipline engineering firms will have fewer phase task codes than architectural firms do, while combination architectural/interior design/space planning/furniture sale companies will have an obvious need for more.

FORMAT

For our purposes we have found it advantageous to assign a maximum of a four-digit number to the combination phase task code. You must be careful not to burden your staff with having to remember unnecessarily long numbers in filling out their time sheets properly. The four-digit phase task code gives you the information you need, and its format makes it easy to remember because of large logical groupings.

The four-digit number is divided into two parts: two digits for the phase and two digits for the task. The phase and the task are separated by a decimal point. Naturally other separators could be used, such as hyphens, asterisks, slashes, or commas. The advantage of using the decimal point is that it remains numeric and thus can maintain a numerical rather than an alphabetical order. This is especially important when working with computers because of the way they sort and alphabetize. Also computers can function more efficiently, faster, and with less memory requirements when working with numbers.

The following is a short example of some phase task codes:

1.0	Predesign services (the phase)
1.01	Administration
1.02	Site selection
1.03	Survey
1.04	Preliminary planning
1.05	Client conferences
2.0	Feasibility study (the phase)
2.01	Administration

2.02	Site selection
2.03	Survey report analysis
2.04	Market analysis
2.05	Client conferences
2.06	Presentation
20.0	Time off (the phase)
20.01	Sick leave
20.02	Vacation
20.03	Comp time
21.0	Marketing (the phase)
21.01	General marketing
21.02	Brochures
21.03	Printing
21.04	Presentation

Notice how common tasks for most phases were assigned the same task part of the number. Client conferences is always the .05 of the phase. Of course this is not a requirement and sometimes it may be difficult to achieve totally, but it certainly makes organization and familiarity with the phase task codes easier for the staff.

Also notice that even though we allocated up to a four-digit number for the phase task code, all four digits were not required. There are some obvious common limitations you should be aware of.

1.0	Phase
1.1	Task
1.2	Task
1.3	Task
1.4	Task
1.5	Task
1.6	Task
1.7	Task
1.8	Task
1.9	Task
1.10	Task

The above example has some serious problems. Numerically 1.1 and 1.10 are the same number. Depending on the computer system you are using you may have a conflict. The above method would effectively limit you on most systems to no more than 9 tasks within any one phase, whereas 1.01 instead of 1.1 permits 99 phases with up to 99 tasks within any one phase.

USES

Phase task codes of course are limited only by the imagination and the needs of the people using them. The following are some of the ways the phase task code is going to be used in this book.

Time Accounting

By using phase task codes, the staff can account, on their time sheets, for all time during the period established. In addition to information concerning projects, hours, etc., they can also indicate the phase task code that best describes what they were doing during that period or block of time. Every change of phase task code is on a different time line.

Time can then be compiled according to what the staff was doing rather than just for whom they were doing it, and analyses can then be done on staff time use.

Billing

If properly done, the description of the phase can be tied to the specific work performed on a given project. Thus, if you are doing surveying work, naturally you will be able to provide (if even only internally) detailed information on what was done, which can be reflected on your bill to your client. This is useful information as backup for hourly billing; it also provides justification for the percentage completed on any phase of a project.

Budgeting, Bidding, and Estimating

There are some jobs that are too large in scope to be swallowed as a whole. It is a time-honored rule that no matter how big the job is, it can be handled if taken in small chunks. This is the basic theory behind phase task codes. They provide you with the ability to digest and look at a project in small manageable parts. This is why it is essential on projects of any substance that they be budgeted by phases. In this way you can more properly evaluate how many hours and how much manpower it will take to complete a phase. When the phases are put together you will have the estimate for the project.

If the preliminary estimates are too high, you can then see what can be cut in an orderly manner rather than just cutting by 10 percent on the whole job.

Job Costing

Job costing goes hand in hand with budgeting. Once the hard part of budgeting, bidding, and estimating are out of the way job costing is easy. You now have to live within those budgets. By analyzing your costs by individual phases and by establishing percentages of each phase to the overall project, you can see more easily exactly how a project is progressing. This permits you to make projections and gives you a steering mechanism to adjust the project and make it profitable before it is too late.

Special Areas

Phase task codes enable you to track special areas of interest without setting up a specific project number. These areas might be marketing, legal considerations, internal renovations, or anything that requires a substantial amount of time that might need to be analyzed or watched closely. Many firms set a specific phase called special areas and use the tasks for the actual areas within the phase.

Payroll

Although you will not actually pay by phase task code, allocating all leave time to a specific phase, such as time off, will permit you to quickly organize and retrieve leave for your staff. The phase task codes also indirectly affect the payroll itself. So that you can properly apply labor costs to your general ledger, salaries and hourly payrolls should be split into direct and indirect payroll dollars. Phase task codes can assist you in doing this.

General Ledger

The phase task code is not necessarily used in your general ledger, but it has a very direct effect on its outcome and on its future analysis. Since payroll divides dollars into direct and indirect, they will be picked up as such in the general ledger. This will permit you to do some interesting ratios and analyses, which are described later in the book.

Historical Analysis

Changes in the value of money from one year to another make the cost of doing a specific type of project in one year almost meaningless in another. One of the things that does not change, unless automation is introduced, is the hours it takes to do like work.

In order to do budgeting, estimating, and bidding, you need to have some idea of the hours it will take to do the job. Of course each project is different, but without accurate historical records it is difficult to go with anything other than your years of experience and general gut feelings, which unfortunately often tend to ignore reality, reinforce prejudices, and obstruct change. There is also no way to account for changes in trends or such factors as automation through computers, word processing, and CAD systems.

Those who rely on experience alone also tend to view the projects of the past as a whole. They have no way of breaking them down into their phases. The result is that projects that are similar in nature but different in scope may present unusual problems. Phase task codes offer the solution. By using historical time broken down by phases it is possible, using a computer, to search this time and see, historically, exactly how much time it did take to do phase 3, for example, on a specific size and type of project. The possibilities for analysis and securing true empirical information upon which to make decisions about your company increase greatly.

HELPFUL HINTS

1. It is important to separate your direct phases from your indirect phases. Since the AIA has traditionally used the first nine phases as direct phases, architectural firms, and those doing business with architects, may want to begin this way. We suggest starting indirect phases at least in the 20s. This will give you 10 additional direct phases if you wish to add some for your own purposes later.
2. Place a list of the phase task codes on the back of your time sheets. This is far more convenient than just providing a flip book. Remember that the easier you make the system for your staff, the more they will use it properly.
3. Keep your phase task codes to a minimum. There is a natural tendency to create long and elaborate lists of phase task codes, most of which are rarely if ever used. They should be well thought out and tailored to each company. Even if you are an architect, do not simply take the AIA phase task codes and decide these are yours. Choose only the ones that you are going to be using, and of course, use their numbers if they fit in with your system.
4. Keep in mind possible joint ventures with other members of your profession. The more consistency the A/E industry can bring to its business, the better for all.
5. Decide on what is best for your firm and stick to it. Even if a total revamp might improve something, you are generally much better off staying with what you have than constantly changing. This, of course, is a very loose rule and must be tempered with a huge dose of common sense.
6. Remember that one of the purposes and uses of the phase task code is job costing. You are usually better off to apply the cost to a job, if possible, than to apply it to general overhead. Remember that your ratios and future analyses will be more accurate if you can allocate most of your costs to specific projects when the choice legitimately occurs.
7. Many firms have an additional services phase. This phase is used in billing when a contract (generally a flat fee contract) has been established. Work above and beyond the contract is coded using a task within additional services. If you do not

have a computer, this is an easy and efficient mechanism for taking care of a very complex problem and facilitating the tracking of time for two types of work on the same project. (Firms with computers, which make it easier to track and separate, will not find this phase as useful.)

As you can see from the discussion in this chapter, phase task codes are an essential ingredient in any organizational structure. No firm is too small to begin using phase task codes. Time is the primary resource available to A/E firms. Because it is as valuable as any commodity, time must have the same internal control set up for analysis, budgeting, and allocation as the money in your bank.

Time Accounting

There is an abundant amount of literature on time management—the proper use of time for the most productivity—and it is, in fact, probably one of the most important management tools. As previously indicated, however, we are not concerned here with the management of time. Therefore we use the term *time accounting* because it is much more descriptive of what we are discussing here.

Time accounting is the vehicle that creates the base of information for virtually everything we do. If the phase task code is the essential building block, it is time accounting that provides the catalyst for organizing information out of separate pieces of data. Time accounting is an organized methodology used in accounting for the most valuable resource available to A/E firms—time.

The source document for time accounting is the time sheet. Although time sheets may differ in appearance, they should all contain the same essential elements, as will be described in this chapter.

One question many firms have about time sheets concerns frequency. Some prefer to use time sheets on a weekly basis, others bimonthly, and still others daily. There are advantages to all cycle types. The important thing to remember about the cycle is that it must be coordinated with the other aspects of your business office. Some considerations are job costing, payroll, client billing, and your general ledger. For example, since your payroll depends on your time sheets, it would be foolish to cycle them on the 1st and the 15th if your payroll schedule is every other week. Also if monthly job costing reports are important to you, weekly time sheets cause a problem since you will be either beginning or ending on short or long uneven weeks.

Keep in mind that any time sheet should have one, and only one, date that represents the time period. Generally, it is the last day of the period, as in "Time Sheet Ending . . ."

Assuming you have solved any problems concerning synchronization, we turn now to some of the pros and cons concerning the different cycles.

WEEKLY TIME SHEETS

One of the biggest problems with the weekly time sheet is that it does not correspond with the exact day of the end of the month. This causes real problems with payroll unless you are on a weekly or every other week cycle.

If you bill your clients on a monthly basis you could have a problem coordinating your billing cutoff date with your time sheet. Remember that the time sheet is going to be the source document for billing. Therefore the cutoff date for billing will have to rotate to correspond with the weekly time sheet.

Depending on your payroll, job costing requirements, and other considerations, your time may physically cover two months. For example, if you pay every week or every other week, there will be many occasions where the Friday or Fridays ending the week will split the month and you will wind up with part of your time in one month and part in another. This may or may not be a problem, depending on your organization.

Weekly time sheets are very difficult to coordinate exactly with your general ledger. Most general ledgers cycle monthly, and depending on the extent to which you attempt to accrue labor costs within a given month or accrue work in progress, you may have difficulty coordinating time with the end of any given month.

Many firms have come up with solutions to the above problems in order to make the weekly time sheet work. The short or long week is one solution. This means you have weekly time sheets during most of the month and a short or long beginning or ending week in order to round out the month. If you use this method be certain that you are not on a weekly or biweekly payroll schedule because you have really modified the weekly time sheet to coordinate with a calendar month.

The weekly time sheet is not all that bleak. There are many firms that use it because it also carries with it some distinct advantages. With weekly time sheets you get much more timely reports than with longer cycles. If you need information about a project on a weekly basis, it does you little good to cycle your time sheets on the 1st and 15th of the month.

Weekly time sheets may give you better control. There is a

rule that the longer the time sheet cycle, the less accurate the time sheet. Human nature being what it is, we all tend to procrastinate. If you know that you do not have to turn in your time sheets for 15 days, you are not inclined to write things down as often. As a result, on many occasions the time sheets are a product of memory. This, of course, can inadvertently cost you or your client money unnecessarily.

BIWEEKLY TIME SHEETS

The biweekly, or every other week, time sheet serves virtually no useful purpose. It has all of the disadvantages of the weekly time sheet and almost none of the advantages. Its only advantage is that there possibly is a little less paperwork.

BIMONTHLY TIME SHEETS

A bimonthly time sheet is submitted twice a month. The most common period covers the 1st to the 15th and the 16th to the 31st (or end of a given month). As with other time sheets, you should have a single date that represents the entire period, for example, the period ending the 15th or the 31st.

Your cutoff billing date must correspond with either of the two ending period dates in the month. This is not a serious problem for most firms because they tend to bill on the 1st or at the end of each month. If, however, yours is a more innovative billing cycle—the 22nd of each month, for example—you will have a problem. Most firms whose billing cycle is early in the month will have a cutoff date of the 15th rather than the end of the month.

With bimonthly time sheets you tend to get less timely reports because, naturally, these cannot be generated until the time sheets are in. A further problem is that, as discussed above, the longer the period, the less accurate time sheets tend to be.

One other consequence, of course, is that your payroll schedule must correspond to the bimonthly dates. All this simply means is that you may not pay weekly or every other week.

The bimonthly time sheet corresponds with the end of each month. This carries with it all of the advantages that were dis-

Bimonthly Time Sheet

Name ______________ Emp. # ______ Period ______________

Project #	Phase Task	Code	Description	1	2	3	4	5	6	7	8	9	10	11	12	13	14	15		Total
				16	17	18	19	20	21	22	23	24	25	26	27	28	29	30	31	
TOTALS																				

advantages with weekly time sheets. Also, accrual or modified accrual, which would require coordination with the general ledger, is not required. This makes this method very attractive.

MONTHLY TIME SHEETS

Monthly time sheets are used mainly by companies that are on a manual system. Naturally, this system has all of the advantages of time sheets that correspond with the end of the month, but it does force your payroll into a monthly schedule.

Firms using a strictly manual system can benefit greatly from the monthly time sheet, if only in the amount of paperwork this system eliminates. If, however, your firm has a computer, the disadvantages of less accuracy and less timely reports far outweigh the reduction in paperwork since the computer does most of the work for you.

DAILY TIME SHEETS

This type of time accounting should be attempted only with a computer and, even then, with a great deal of caution. The paper generated will be tremendous in a medium or large firm. Naturally there are no coordination considerations since the daily time sheet can coordinate with any cycle. The giant benefits of daily time sheets are extreme accuracy and timeliness. Maintaining this type of time accounting, however, usually costs the firm a tremendous amount, not only in terms of money, but also time and employee resources.

PARTS OF A TIME SHEET

Date

Each time sheet should have one single date that represents the time sheet period. This is usually the date of the last day of the time sheet period. If you use a computer, this will be the key date for all searches and interfaces.

Employee Number

Each employee should be assigned a number and care should be taken never to reuse that number. This is especially important for historical purposes.

Employee Classification

An employee classification describes basically what the employee does. This is used in time accounting but is of more importance in client billing. Some examples of employee classifications are:

Principal
Project architect-engineer
Designer
Technician
Draftsman
Support staff
Surveyor

It is not necessary to restrict yourself to only one classification per employee. Even though each employee has a general classification that is used most of the time, it is not uncommon in smaller firms for each staff member to put on many hats.

Type

If you are using a computer you should always have a free field to use for your individual requirements. Generally speaking the type field is tied to the project but for many different purposes. One of the most popular uses of the type table is to define project types. The following are some examples.

Governmental Forms 254/255: This is especially useful when you are bidding on government contracts that require you to report, via Forms 254/255, your other projects of the same size and scope as the one you are currently bidding on.

Discipline: This can be used by multidisciplined firms in order to allocate time to each discipline, for example MEP (mechanical/electrical/plumbing), structural, civil, etc.

Project Size and Scope: This is another commonly used heading under project types, and unless your firm has a special need that far exceeds the benefits of this heading, it is recommended by far. The benefits of the project size and scope category have to do with historical analysis—how much time historically has been spent on a given type of project for a given phase. You can use this information in bidding, cost estimating, job costing, and so on.

Project size and scope refers to the type of project being undertaken. Typically this heading might include such project types as:

Commercial
Residential
Multifamily
Condominiums
Subdivisions
Class A projects

Client: This is used if you have a need to organize your projects according to the client. When firms have one or more clients who have several projects each, many times it is very helpful to be able to search time sheet data and group it by projects done for a specific client.

Project Manager: Extremely large firms may wish to use this field to organize their projects according to the project manager, making it easier to run, sort, and distribute reports.

Project Number

There are many methods of structuring project numbers. The actual structure is not as important as is making sure that each project is given a unique number and is accounted for.

The following are examples of project number systems:

87001: The first two numbers represent the year in which the project was begun. The 001 is the first project of the year. Subsequent projects are numbered sequentially.

70701: The first number represents the year (the 7 represents 1987). The next two numbers are the month in which the project began. The last two numbers represent the sequential order of projects per month.

87001.01: This numbering system is basically like the one in the first example but includes a decimal suffix that may have a variety of meanings. The most common use of the suffix is for projects that are in some way related to an original project for a client.

Depending upon your needs the project number can represent a myriad of meanings: type of billing, marketing projects, or in-house projects are just a few of the possibilities. Some of these are more or less important depending on your organizational structure and system flexibility. As you will see there are several ways to get at the same information. All of it does not have to be encompassed in the project number.

Phase Task Code

Refer to the section on phase task codes.

Time

Time generally should be filled out in tenths. We have found the most practical minimum unit is the quarter hour. Although six minutes (one-tenth of an hour) is also a multiple of one hour, it is just too short a period for practical application, and ten-minute increments do not convert easily to tenths. Half-hour increments lose too much time (often it is not reasonable to bill for a full half hour).

Billing Rate

The billing rate is included on the time sheet only for those projects that are billed on an hourly basis. Although client billing will be discussed in more detail later, we should mention here that there are two types of projects: hourly billing and flat fee. On some occasions a flat fee project may include additional services that are to be billed on an hourly basis. This combined type of contract or billing mode requires that the person processing the time sheets know which hours are to be billed on an hourly basis and which hours on a percentage of the project completed.

Direct or Indirect Flag

The time sheet should in some manner differentiate between indirect and direct time. This may be done either by separating the direct time and the indirect time or by marking or flagging each individual line as either direct or indirect.

Payroll Flag

In many situations, time sheets must be kept on individuals who are not considered part of the payroll. Therefore you should have a way of differentiating between those time sheets that will eventually become part of the payroll and those that will not. This is especially important if you have contract labor time.

Billing Flag

This is used to indicate whether the hour is to be billed or not, and will permit an easy division of time: flat fee, hourly time, and time that is hourly because it is an additional service on a flat fee project.

Each of the above fields can be easily filled in to blanks on the time sheet. Whenever the value of a field changes because of a change in project, type, phase task code, and so on, a new line can be established. On a subsequent day or for the same day, if that line is appropriate it can be reused and the time put in the appropriate days position on the time sheet.

At the end of the period, the time sheet is first totaled down, per day, then across the individual time lines. Both figures should be the same. The individual doing the compilation of the time sheet, whether by hand or on a computer, will only have to be concerned with the totals for check figures.

As indicated previously, one of the problems with the bimonthly time sheet is the lack of accuracy because of the length of time between cycles. However, a bimonthly time sheet could be checked more often than every 15 days. For example, it could be turned in two times per bimonthly period. In other words, if the time sheet dates are the 1st and 15th, the cycle could be broken into 1–7, 8–15, 16–22, and 23–31 (or end of month). This method has the advantages of weekly time sheets and is easier to keep since you do not have short and long weeks if you wish to keep it within a calendar month. Cutoff periods for billing may be on the 22nd, which helps in getting bills to clients prior to the 1st, and is still more or less within the last week of the month or close to it, unlike the 15th.

TIME ANALYSIS

Although difficult without a computer, it is extremely important to be able to analyze time for management purposes. This requires the ability to ask the computer questions concerning the time that is available in the data base. This search capability permits you to combine search keys in order to focus in on a combination of specific time lines within any period of time.

The ability to search your time data base opens up innumerable possibilities. We have discussed previously the historical importance of time. By properly asking the computer for the time spent on a specific phase of a given project type, you can find out the historical standard for your particular company, which can help you in bidding, estimating, and budgeting.

Time accounting also offers an excellent method of auditing time for correctness. A concise printout, properly sorted and distributed for review, can aid in eliminating obvious mistakes.

Many times job costing will give you information concerning the labor cost of a project by phase but will not necessarily tell you why there is an overrun. Time accounting searches can indicate which hours were performed on the project, by whom, and under what classification. Another possible use might be to isolate billable hours from flat fee hours for a given time period. As you can see, the exact information you can acquire from time accounting will depend on what exactly you need to know. As we progress through other aspects of management, you will see just how easily and quickly a proper search of the time sheet data base through time accounting can answer a multitude of questions. Time accounting opens up many management techniques that can help you and your firm increase profits and become more efficient.

Utilization Rates

DIRECT AND INDIRECT TIME

An understanding of direct and indirect time is essential for the proper management of an A/E firm because such a designation of time has an influence in the following areas:

Utilization rates
General ledger
Overhead rates
Hourly rate multipliers

Direct time is simply that time which is attributable to a project from which you receive money. Indirect time is all other time; that is, time not attributable to projects from which you receive money.

Often the terms billable and nonbillable time are used synonymously with direct and indirect time. Since there are so many ways of billing a project, this can become confusing. For example, even though a project is billed on a flat fee basis, it still generates money. Thus, although each hour worked is not directly billable, time to that project is direct. Using our terms—direct and indirect—will help you keep the two types of time straight.

DIRECT TIME TO TOTAL TIME RATIO

Let us now look at how time designations can be used to give us meaningful reports. The time sheets provide total direct and indirect hours for each employee as well as the direct and indirect breakdown of the total hours of the office as a whole. This information can be used to calculate a series of ratios, the first of which is the utilization rate. Two formulas can be used to establish the utilization rate. The first formula is:

$$U = DT/TT,$$

where U is the utilization rate, DT is the direct time, and TT is the total time worked by the employee. The second formula for establishing the utilization rate is:

$$U = DT/AT,$$

where U is the utilization rate, DT is the direct time, and AT is the available time.

An example will illustrate the difference between the above two formulas. Say that the available time is a standard 40-hour work week. An employee works 60 hours, 20 hours of which are indirect and 40 hours direct. If the employee is paid by the hour for every hour worked, then you should use the first formula for utilization rate:

$$U = 40/60.$$

The utilization rate is 67 percent. But if the employee is salaried and therefore not paid for the additional 20 hours worked, you should use the second formula:

$$U = 40/40.$$

The utilization rate is 100 percent, meaning that the employer received all of the time he paid for as direct. You can have a utilization rate above 100 percent.

If employees are paid overtime on an hourly basis at a higher rate than straight time, the utilization rate will be slightly skewed as a result of the overtime.

It is important to note here that there is no attempt to correlate actual dollars spent to the utilization rate since two individuals each with a 73 percent utilization rate, for example, can be paid different hourly rates.

Invariably, a firm will have a number of payroll policies in effect and most offices tend to mix them. Therefore the utilization rate should not be viewed as an absolute. Norms such as a 65 to 68 percent utilization rate for an office as break-even should be viewed with a high degree of skepticism.

This is not to say that the utilization rate is not valuable. It is an extremely valuable management tool, but one that is generally misused. It is also not an absolute determiner of profit/loss: that is the job of the general ledger. Actually it is a barometer, one that points to trouble.

Each individual has a normal utilization rate. These norms for individuals can be tracked using spread sheets. What the manager needs to do is to look for changes in the norms—up or down. These changes point to potential problems and should be investigated through time accounting to help the project manager discover their causes.

Even an abnormally high utilization rate can be a potential problem. For example, a marketing individual may be pulled off to work on a rush job. Even though this may be necessary in the short run, it may cause problems in the long run if it occurs consistently and future projects do not materialize.

An abnormally high office utilization rate coupled with lots of overtime could indicate it is time to hire extra personnel or additional support staff. Each abnormality should be analyzed and satisfied. Remember the purpose of the utilization rate is to point to potential problems before they become major ones.

General Ledger

CHART OF ACCOUNTS

It is not our purpose to teach accounting here. Every A/E firm should have the advice of an individual competent in accounting. Our goal is to illustrate the method of organizing your chart of accounts to give you managerial information from your general ledger. The general ledger consists of financial accounting books and the individual accounts.

We are going to skip any discussion of assets, liabilities, and capital here and are not going to concern ourselves with company form, such as corporation, partnership, or sole proprietorship, except where it concerns salaries. Our discussion will be limited to revenue and expenditure accounts, those accounts that make up the profit/loss statement.

In the traditional accounting structure, an attempt is made to divide the expenditures into variable and fixed expenses for the purpose of break-even analysis and to produce ratios of expenditures to net revenue less cost of goods sold. This, of course, works well for organizations that make a profit on goods. And if your firm also sells furniture, for example, you will need a modified section of your chart of accounts to take this into consideration.

Most A/E firms, however, sell time and expertise, not goods. And although we can adapt a portion of the chart of accounts (see pages 30–32) to reflect the cost of reimbursable items, the main emphasis should not be on variable and fixed expenditures, but on direct and indirect expenses. You will notice a high correlation between the two, which is a small bonus, but the main emphasis should be on direct and indirect.

Your chart of accounts should have at least two payroll accounts: direct and indirect. Naturally you may have more payroll accounts within each group. The point is that most employees should have payroll expenses distributed to two general ledger payroll accounts. Labor costs make up the major expenses of any organization and should be properly allocated so that any analysis will have validity.

The following is a sample of a complete chart of accounts. It is meant to be representative of the format used to collect information needed by A/E firms for direct and indirect expenses. It should be adapted for your particular needs and should be reviewed by your accountant.

Chart of Accounts

Account	Description
1000	Assets
1100	Cash
1111	Cash, Checking
1112	Cash, Savings
1113	Petty Cash
1199	Total Cash
1200	Accounts Receivable
1211	A/R, Trade Contracts
1212	A/R, Other
1299	Total Accounts Receivable
1300	Fixed Assets
1311	Furniture and Fixtures
1312	Accumulated Depreciation, Furniture and Fixtures
1313	Transportation Equipment
1314	Accumulated Depreciation, Transportation Equipment
1315	Leasehold Improvements
1316	Accumulated Depreciation, Leasehold Improvements
1399	Total Fixed Assets
1600	Other Assets
1611	Deposits
1612	Prepaid Interest
1613	Prepaid Insurance
1699	Total Other Assets
1999	Total Assets
2000	Liabilities
2111	Accounts Payable
2141	Federal Withholding
2142	Payroll Deductions
2143	State Withholdings
2144	FUTA Payable

Account	Description
2145	State Unemployment Payable
2151	Interest Payable
2411	Note Payable (Name of Lender)
2412	Note Payable (Name of Lender)
2999	Total Liabilities
3000	Capital
3111	Capital Stock
3311	Retained Earnings
3511	Current Earnings
3998	Total Capital
3999	Total Liabilities and Capital
5000	Revenue
5111	Professional Contract Fees
5112	Noncontract Fees
5119	Other Revenue
5999	Total Revenue
6000	Expenses
6100	Direct Expenses
6111	Direct Salaries, Officer
6112	Direct Salaries, Other
6121	Reimbursable Direct Expenses
6141	Reimbursable Consultants
6161	Nonreimbursable Direct Expenses
6181	Nonreimbursable Consultants
6299	Total Direct Expenses
6500	Indirect Expenses
6511	Indirect Salaries, Officer
6512	Indirect Salaries, Other
6521	Auto Expenses
6522	Bank Charges
6523	Periodicals
6524	Nondirect Consulting Fees
6525	Contributions
6526	Dues and Memberships
6527	Employee Benefits
6528	Insurance

(continued)

Chart of Accounts (continued)

Account	Description
6529	Life Insurance
6530	Legal Expenses
6531	Accounting Expenses
6532	Penalties
6533	Printing
6534	Office Supplies
6535	Matching FICA Taxes
6536	FUTA Taxes
6537	State Unemployment Taxes
6538	Postage
6539	Rent
6540	Utilities
6541	Repairs and Maintenance
6542	Seminars, Education
6543	Telephone
6544	Travel and Promotion
6545	Depreciation Expense
6546	State Corporation Taxes
6547	Federal Corporation Taxes
6699	Total Indirect Expenses
6999	Total Expenses
8999	Net Income

A direct expense is any expense that can be allocated to a specific project. If time accounting is properly handled and direct and indirect time allocated, direct and indirect labor costs should take care of themselves. Examples of direct expenses are:

Direct salaries
Consultant costs
Direct travel
Contract labor
Reproductions
Postage and freight
Project-related telephone

One thing you should note is that some of these expenditures may have an indirect counterpart, such as in travel, telephone, and postage. And even though these are the major direct expenses, there is almost always a need for a miscellaneous direct expenses account.

Another useful tool is to further divide the direct expenses into reimbursable and nonreimbursable. This is so that reimbursable revenue can be paired with reimbursable expenses as required.

On a true allocative basis the direct costs of payroll should properly be allocated as a direct expenditure. This is very difficult to do and for our analysis is not necessary. We prefer the more pragmatic approach of allocating all costs of payroll to indirect expenses. Some of these accounts would include:

Matching FICA
Employment taxes
FUTA (federal unemployment taxes)
Workmen's compensation insurance

The one major complication is the partnership or sole proprietorship that does not reflect owner draw as a salary expense. This is solved in one of two ways:

1. Establish a set of special direct and indirect payroll expenditure accounts and post draws to these accounts. This will give you a better picture of the profit/loss of the company with the fair value of the owner labor reflected as an expenditure. Draws above this fair value should be debited from the capital accounts. Remember this method is for management reports only. For true financial reporting, such as to the IRS, these accounts should be closed to capital.
2. The second method is to set up a direct and indirect capital draw for the fair value of the labor performed by the owner. If you use this method, remember to include these balances with expenditures in calculating the overhead rate.

The following are two complete sample charts of accounts for revenues and expenditures. These are only samples for illustration purposes. Please have someone knowledgeable in accounting actually set up your chart of accounts.

Chart of Accounts—A

- Revenue
  - Professional fee revenue
  - Reimbursable revenue
  - Other revenue
  - Total revenue
- Expenses
- Direct Expenses
  - Salary, principals
  - Salary, employees
  - Consultants
  - Reproductions
  - Direct travel
  - Photography
  - Miscellaneous direct expenses
- Total Direct Expenses
- Indirect Expenses
  - Salary, principals
  - Salary, employees
  - Advertising
  - Depreciation expense
  - Insurance
  - Payroll taxes
  - Interest expense
  - Legal
  - Accounting
  - Repairs and maintenance
  - Rent
  - Postage/shipping/freight
  - Office supplies
  - Continuing education
- Total Indirect Expenses
- Total Expenses
- Net Income

Chart of Accounts—B

- Revenue
  - Professional fee revenue
  - Reimbursable revenue

Direct Expenses
- Direct salary, principals
- Direct salary, employees
- Consultants
- Reproductions
- Direct travel
- Photography
- Miscellaneous direct expenses

Total Revenue from Operations

Indirect Expenses
- Salary, principals
- Salary, employees
- Advertising
- Depreciation expense
- Insurance
- Payroll taxes
- Interest expense
- Legal
- Accounting
- Repairs and maintenance
- Rent
- Postage/shipping/freight
- Office supplies
- Continuing education

Total Indirect Expenses

Net Income from Operations

Other Revenue
- Interest revenue
- Miscellaneous revenue

Total Other Revenue

Net Income

As you can see the basic difference in the two charts of account is that the second tends to pattern itself after cost of goods sold examples; it gives information concerning revenue from operations and matches the cost of revenue. There are, of course, many variations to the above charts. What is essential is that you be able to pull out direct expenses from the general ledger.

Overhead Rate

The overhead rate is an important ratio because it impacts directly on the profitability of the company. The proper calculation and monitoring of the overhead rate is vital as it is used in determining both the hourly rates you should charge and the basis of flat fee calculations. It also is used as an ongoing analysis of profitability per project in job costing.

In order to calculate the overhead rate you will need certain information from the general ledger, which must therefore be organized in such a way as to easily give this information.

The actual formula for the overhead rate is quite easy: total expenses divided by direct salary expenses. But the application of this formula in its pure form can be very misleading because of large consultant fees that are reimbursable. Other items might be the sale of furniture or merchandise. These items can grossly distort the overhead rate and must be subtracted out.

Therefore begin with total expenses and subtract the following:

Total Expenses
– Reimbursable Consultants
– Other Reimbursable Expenses

– Cost of Goods Sold
– Sales Tax Expense

Adjusted Total Expenses
– Direct Labor

Overhead Expenses

You should also subtract anything unique to your company that might skew the results.

Notice that we subtracted direct labor. This may differ from some formulas you have seen, but it is necessary for the way we are going to apply the overhead rate. What we are after is a dollar amount of overhead. Direct labor is not overhead for our calculations. Our final goal is to find out how much profit we must make on each hour cost of labor to meet the rest of our expenses or overhead. Therefore we want to be able to multiply a percentage overhead rate by our direct labor expense and produce this overhead.

Total Expenses = Direct Labor + Overhead

For example:

Total Expenses	15,000
– Reimbursable Consultants	– 4,000
– Other Reimbursable Expenses	– 1,000
Adjusted Total Expenses	10,000
– Direct Labor Expense	– 4,000
Overhead Expense	6,000

Overhead expense divided by direct labor expense equals overhead rate:

6,000/4,000 = 1.50 or 150%

Let us calculate back to see if we are right and to see the relationship of overhead rate to direct labor:

Adjusted Total Expenses	10,000
Direct Labor	4,000
× Overhead Rate	1.50
Overhead Expense	6,000

Remember our formula: adjusted total expenses equals direct labor plus overhead expense. Thus:

10,000 = 4,000 + 6000

Therefore if you know that your current overhead rate is 150 percent, then you know you must charge an additional $1.50 for every $1.00 cost of direct labor in order to achieve break-even.

Notice an important point here. We did not attempt to give any kind of weight to the employee cost for things such as FICA, leave, health benefits, etc. These items are already included in adjusted total expenses and any attempt to add them to direct labor would subtract them from overhead. Even though the overhead rate would be lower it would be applied against a higher direct labor expense and the results would be the same. Actually you would be a little less accurate because methods such as this attempt to prorate the costs. The first method is precise because it is using actual expense figures.

Now that we know that our overhead rate is 150 percent of direct labor, let us see what our billing rate for a draftsman at $9.00 per hour would be. We will also assume we want a 20 percent profit on our labor cost.

Cost of Employee	9.00/hr.
20% on Cost	1.80/hr.
Overhead Cost (9.00 × 150%)	13.50/hr.
Total Billing Rate	24.30/hr.

For practical purposes we could round this figure out to $25.00 per hour.

Overhead naturally will vary from month to month and especially from one year to the next. If no adjustments are made for these variations, false assumptions will be made in the bidding process, which will be discussed later. At the same time, changing the overhead rate every month can result in wild gyrations because any given month may have unexpected expenses.

We have found that the best solution to this problem is to use a 12-month moving average. This is simply a mean average (total overhead rates of 12 months divided by 12) for one year and becomes your current overhead rate. The next month add the current month to the 12 and subtract the first before dividing so you are always working with the most recent 12 months. This becomes the new current overhead rate.

This method permits you to chart the moving average and to detect trends upward or downward, which is especially important in bidding for flat fee projects. If your overhead is in an upward trend, for example, using the current overhead rate would result in a possible loss for a long-term project.

If you are using a computer for job costing it is important that the overhead be computed each time it is applied rather than saved and accumulated as a permanent dollar amount. The latter method does not allow for the moving average, nor does it permit you to run reports with and/or without overhead.

Bidding (Project Cost Estimating)

We use the term *project cost estimating* here to refer to the costs incurred in performing the professional services for which you are being paid. It does not refer to the cost of construction. Once the A/E costs are properly estimated, the bid (how much your fee will be) is simply your profit added to your cost.

The following are very simplified worksheet examples to illustrate the procedure to be used in cost estimating and bidding. We will elaborate on the worksheet and eventually produce a spread sheet, which may conveniently be used by any of the popular spread sheet computer programs.

The first example shows a method that can be used to calculate a flat rate project.

A	Estimated number of hours	250
B	Average hourly cost	11.40
C	Overhead rate	150%
D	Percent profit	20%
E	Consultants and other direct charges	3,000

We perform the following calculations:

F	Labor cost ($F=A\times B$)	2,850
G	Overhead cost ($G=F\times C$)	4,275
H	Profit ($H=F\times D$)	570
	Bid ($F+G+H+E$)	**$10,695**

Let us compare this method to an hourly project of 250 hours. First we compute our billing rate:

Cost of employee	11.40
20% profit	2.28
Overhead cost	17.10

The billing rate is 30.78 × 250 hours = $7,695, which is exactly the same as the previous method less $3,000 for consultants and other nonreimbursable direct charges.

There is one major difference between the two methods. On an hourly basis you are guaranteed billing for every hour worked. With a flat fee contract you are not paid for an overrun, but at the same time you are rewarded for coming in under budget in terms of hours and dollars.

For flat fee contracts, there is a risk factor that needs to be calculated in, and how great that risk factor will be is determined by how good you are at guessing the number of hours it will take to do the project. If you have no historical data, you are stabbing in the dark. Time accounting can give you this historical perspective. There are two ways you can lose money by using "gut instinct" in place of historical information:

1. *Underbidding:* If it takes you more hours than you estimated you can lose your shirt. Utilization rates may be high, overhead rates may be good, but the dollars are not there to cover the costs.
2. *Overbidding:* This is the secret killer. Profits are eaten away here in lost contracts. You cannot job cost a project you never got. There are usually certain preliminary costs in marketing and possible predesign that are written off to overhead. These costs not only have an impact on the bottom line, as other costs would, but they also carry with them a double whammy. They impact the overhead rate and thus your future bids. This will eventually reduce drastically your ability to compete.

Even with—or better said, especially with—good historical information, a risk factor is necessary. If you are exactly on target with the number of hours, time after time, the risk factor not only guards against your error but should reward you for your efficiency and willingness to take the risk of a flat fee contract. It is also the cost that your client pays for your removing his risk of uncertain fees.

The question arises, Where should this risk factor be applied in our formulas? Unquestionably it should go at the beginning on the estimated number of hours needed to complete the project. This is the only place that the cost of these hours will be properly allocated throughout the formulas. Therefore if you decide on a 10 percent risk factor, you simply add 25 hours to the 250 hours in our example.

Another adjustment that is a must is in the overhead rate. If in your charting of the past year's overhead rates you discover that your company has an upward trend, an adjustment needs to be made here. The trend we are referring to is the increase in the moving average, not in the gross overhead rates from month to month.

For example, if the moving average has increased over the past six months from 140 percent to 160 percent, it has gone up approximately 15 percent over the past six months. If you have a project that is going to last six months or longer, you will underbid the project if you use your current overhead rate and this increase continues at the same or an accelerated rate.

The adjustment should be made as follows. A crude chart should be constructed for six months:

Current Overhead Rate		160%	
Expected Final Rate		184%	(160 + 15%)
Difference		24	
Per Month Expected Increase		4	(24/6)
Month 1	164		
Month 2	168		
Month 3	172		
Month 4	176		
Month 5	180		
Month 6	184		
Total		174	(1,044/6)

Therefore you would use 174 percent instead of 160 percent during your bid estimating for a project expected to last six months. Naturally this formula would be modified depending on the average trend increase and the estimated duration of the project under consideration.

So far we have confined our discussion to the project as a whole. As discussed previously, it is very difficult to work this way, especially on large projects. That is why we divide the projects into phases. In this way we can work with smaller, more understandable aspects of the project. An even more vital reason to divide a large project into phases for bid estimating is that each phase may have some unique features that must be taken into consideration separately.

Although we may be able to average the cost of employees for the organization, it would be more precise if we could get an average cost of employee for each phase of the project. It goes without saying that a surveyor or designer earns a salary different from a draftsman. Other classifications of employees have still other different cost rates. The ideal method of estimating would therefore be to identify the actual individuals who are going to be doing the work and to estimate their actual cost per hour when plugging them into the formulas. Of course for a large organization this can become very time consuming and may never get done. What we are after is a method that not only carries a great deal of accuracy, even though not perfect, but also is simple enough in its application that it will be used consistently.

In most firms there is a classification or group of classifications

SAMPLE SPREAD SHEET

A Phase	B Hours	C Labor/Hr.	D Overhead	E % Profit	F % Total
1	XXX	XX.XX	X.XX	.XX	(formula)
2					
3					
4					
5					
Total					

A. Name of each of the phases of the project.

B. Estimated number of hours you would expect to spend on each phase of the project (remember to add in your risk percentage factor here).

C. Calculated average cost per hour of labor for each phase of the project.

D. Overhead percentage rate. (If it is 150 percent, write it in as 1.50. This should be a constant number in each phase of the project since it is a company-wide figure and the individual phases would not differ. Remember to do your calculations if your company is in an upward trend.)

E. Constant profit percentage. (As with overhead it would be the same for all phases. If it is 20 percent, then it would be written as .20.)

F. The formula that goes in F is as follows: $(B \times C) + (B \times C \times D) + (B \times C \times E)$

of employees who tend to work on a particular phase. And even when there are several groups they usually work a consistent percentage of time in a specific phase in relationship to the other classifications involved. Therefore you should be able to come up with an average labor cost per phase, which you can then apply to all projects.

The above formulas would still apply, but instead of being used only one time for the entire project, they would be used independently for each phase of the project. Each column would then be added up for the project as a whole.

This creates an ideal use for a computer spread sheet because you can do many "what if's," with the computer performing all of the math in a matter of seconds. A hard copy of the bid, containing the necessary information for the files, can then be used for budget figures as the project progresses into job costing.

The spread sheet shown on page 43 will give you your labor cost. Remember to add in the additional cost of nonreimbursable consultants and other direct charges that will make up the final fee bid. Information should be filled out for each phase of the project that is applicable. Totals for *B* and *F* should be calculated.

As you can well imagine there are numerous variations on this spread sheet. Additional columns could be added for each step of the calculations, consultants could be added for each phase, and so on. As you gain more experience with spread sheets, you should experiment with adapting them for your own use. The important thing is that you go through the procedure and secure at least the minimum information that it provides.

Job Costing

Job costing is probably the most misunderstood function in A/E accounting. Most firms see job costing simply as a collection of hours and dollars spent on a project. A few firms actually have budgets and attempt in some manner to relate what is being spent to the budget of the project or the budgets of the phases. All of this is, of course, a start for job costing, and each of these procedures is a necessary component part of the job costing process. But the information is not complete, and the average project manager will not know what he is looking at. Even if you have a computer and it pours out reams of paper, unless you know what you are looking for, the effort is senseless.

THE PURPOSE OF JOB COSTING

Without a solid understanding of the purpose of job costing, the data that you accumulate are not going to do you very much good. The true purpose of job costing can be summed up as the control of hours and dollars performed on a project in order to limit their expenditures to a predetermined budget.

Let us return for a moment to bidding and cost estimating. You have bid out a flat fee contract for $35,000. Through the formulas that we have outlined you have determined that you can perform the scope of this project for a given labor cost, an overhead percentage factor, a percentage profit, and certain non-reimbursable direct charges and consultant costs. You have carefully and completely constructed a budget of hours and dollars for each phase of the project and the numbers all work *before* you get the contract. If you have done all of this, you have created a working plan for the project, which may now be tracked.

In this formula you have basically stated that if you can do the project for a given labor cost, then you will make a predetermined profit. The number of hours needed to perform the phases is *not* a constant. The total labor dollars are the constant. The number of hours is dependent on the labor cost per employee at the time you cost estimate the project. This is a fact that is often missed by many managers. What usually occurs is that the personnel used during the actual production of the project are not the same as those used in the estimation. Sometimes managers will look at a job costing report and consider only hours worked when comparing it to the budget. Their general comment is that they have a given number of hours left to work in that phase. This simply is not true.

The purpose of job costing is simply to perform a fixed fee project for as much or less money than you budget. In doing so not only do you get paid for the work you do, but you are also greatly rewarded for the efficiency of bringing the project in *under* budget. This is the real secret of making money in architecture and engineering.

The question arises, What is the role of hourly projects in job costing. This may come as a shock to most managers, but there is little reason to go to the time and expense to cost out straight hourly projects. If you are losing money on a straight hourly project, you have not done your overhead calculations correctly and thus do not have sound billing rates. This does not mean that you should not know, for historical purposes, how many hours it took to do a phase or type of project. As mentioned previously, this is essential, but it is really part of time accounting, not of job costing.

THE JOB COST SYSTEM

Let us take a look at a good job costing system by answering some common questions and dispelling some of the erroneous ideas about job costing.

1. Must all projects be job costed?

In most firms, job costing is a waste of time. It is not part of the financial statements of the company. Remember that job costing is a management tool that helps you control projects and bring them in under budget so that the reduced costs will increase the profits of the project.

If every project your firm undertakes is a large fixed-fee one, then by all means job cost them all. But if yours is like most firms, you will have several significantly large projects that mean the difference in profitability for the firm as a whole, and you will have many small, short projects or those that are straight hourly. Job costing all projects can be a massive undertaking that can stretch valuable resources to the limit. And even with a computer, this could produce such massive amounts of paper that the managers may never look at the data. It is much better to be selective and spend your time where it matters the most: on the significant projects that can make or break your firm. And watch them like a hawk.

2. Are budgets necessary? All my firm wants to know is how many hours and dollars we have spent on a project.

Creating a budget for a fixed-fee project is not specifically a function of job costing. You create the budget when you do the cost estimating in order to bid out the project. If you have not gone through this procedure, how do you know how much to bid? Here again you are stabbing in the dark.

Job costing is a management tool to control costs. Knowing you have spent 50 hours on a phase tells you, in and of itself, absolutely nothing. Without a budget you have nothing to measure against.

3. Is the percentage of the budgeted hours spent important?

Unfortunately this is one of the most worthless pieces of information available to the manager. It tells you nothing at all.

If you budget 70 hours for a phase and are 35 hours into that phase of the project, you cannot say that you have completed 50 percent of the phase. Rarely is this even close to reality. How far along a project really is will rarely correlate exactly with the percentage of the budget used. In fact you do not want it to. You want to better the budget. But as soon as you put in the variable percentage completed, you have given management meaningful information. In the above example, it would make a big difference to know that 90 percent of the project is complete after 35 hours rather than 30 percent. Now the fact that you have used 35 of the 70 available hours has real meaning.

4. What is a budget variance?

A variance is the percentage that you are off budget. Of course to know if you are off budget it is necessary to know how many hours will be used by the end of the project. Once you know this, it is simple to compute how much over- or underbudget you are.

In order to manage projects it is necessary to make a projection on the final outcome of the project before the project ends. These projections require only two pieces of information: number of hours spent and percentage of project actually completed.

This is an easy calculation. If you have spent 35 hours and the project is 20 percent complete, 35/.20 = 175, which is the total number of hours that will be spent by the time it is finished. Naturally, the more complete the project is the more accurate the projection will become. Next, simply compute the percentage difference between the projected 175 hours and the budgeted hours, which gives you the variance in hours for the phase. This is one of the factors that should be constantly monitored.

5. *Is it necessary to compute the variance both in hours and in dollars?*

Yes, definitely. If your average budgeted rate per hour is $10 and your actual current rate is $12, you may have a good variance in hours and a very bad variance in dollars because you are using more expensive personnel than you budgeted for. Both of these variances are important.

The dollar projection is the product of the projected hours times the average current rate per hour of expenditure. This dollar projection is then measured against the budget.

6. *How should overhead be handled?*

As indicated previously, the overhead rate should be computed monthly and as a 12-month moving average. This is your current overhead rate. Overhead is applied in inverse proportion to direct labor. Therefore if your overhead rate is 150 percent, you must add $1.50 in overhead for every $1.00 of direct labor.

Since you are using a 12-month moving average for the overhead rate, the overhead should be computed for each job costing report rather than being saved and accumulated. Accumulating overhead does not allow for the moving average nor does it permit you to run reports without overhead.

7. *What is the relationship of direct charges and reimbursable charges in job costing?*

In bidding and cost estimating, the nonreimbursable direct charges are added into the final contract bid amount. Therefore these consultants are part of the fee. The final profit/loss of a given project is the total fee of the contract less the labor expense and the nonreimbursable direct charges. Since the reimbursable direct charges are not part of the project fee, they should not be subtracted.

8. What is an adjusted budget?

Let us assume that your budget calls for $100 at $10 per hour. Therefore you can afford to spend 10 hours in order to stay within your budget. Remember that the $100 is the constant, not the number of hours. If you use personnel that cost you $5 per hour, you can afford 20 hours and still stay within the same $100 budget. Conversely, if you use personnel that cost $20 per hour, your budget must be cut to 5 hours. This is called the adjusted budget. Every job costing report should measure the average rate per hour and thus readjust the hourly budget.

In actuality, the adjusted budget in hours becomes the real budget, making it more important than the original budget. Budget balances and comparisons should always be measured against the adjusted budget of hours.

Paradoxically, job costing is the one single activity an architect or engineer can engage in that can produce enormous profits. Unfortunately, because of the massive amount of time required to do job costing manually, it is often ignored. We cannot repeat too often, however, that there is one major way to make big money in architecture and engineering: Bid the project on a flat fee basis and bring the project in substantially under budget.

Client Billing

Client billing is often a complicated, difficult, and dreaded procedure for many A/E firms. How complicated the billing process becomes is directly related to how complicated and nonstandard the contracts you write with your clients are. At the same time your ability to be flexible in your contractual terms is what gives you the ability to be competitive.

It is our contention that nothing need be complicated if broken down into its component parts and digested in small bites—one reason for phases. Therefore, let us look at the different types of billing methods available to A/E firms.

There are basically only two main types of invoicing methods, several variations of each, as well as combinations of the two. The two types are:

A. Hourly rates
B. Flat fees

Under each of these are the variations:

A. Hourly Rates
    1. Straight hourly by:
        a. Classification
        b. Employee
    2. Hourly to maximum by:
        a. Classification
        b. Employee
B. Flat Fees
    1. Single contract amount
    2. Percent of phase completed
    3. Percent of construction cost
    4. Square feet
C. Hybrids

Now let us examine these one at a time. In doing so we will look at the advantages and disadvantages of each as well as some of the pitfalls in the methods and the accounting involved.

HOURLY RATES

This method of billing and contracting with clients is by far the safest. But in most cases it does not afford you the opportunity of being rewarded for efficient work. The biggest drawback to hourly billing revolves around not billing for the actual hours worked. Many times, of course, this is necessary because there is such an extensive overrun that the client will not stand for it. In such a case, it is possible to take a loss on a strictly hourly project.

What is important in an hourly billing project is that a careful analysis has been performed on your overhead rate and that you have computed an appropriate billing rate for each employee. Most firms tend to bill by classification of employee, such as design architect, surveyor, draftsman, and so on. Each billing rate should always be tied in some way to the actual employees that will be performing the work. If general classifications are to have their own billing rate, you should try to average the cost of the various employees that are part of that classification.

FLAT FEES

The flat fee contract is a completely different animal. You have the opportunity for rich rewards if the project is bid correctly and your work is performed efficiently. At the same time the client is protected from overruns. The flat fee contract does have the potential of losing money if proper controls are not exercised.

From an accounting point of view, the flat fee contract is handled completely differently—from first billing all the way through retainers, payments, and partial payments in receivables. As indicated above, payment is normally made as the progress of the project is reported to the client and a percentage completed. In small flat fee contracts, many times there is only one payment, the single contract amount, which is made upon completion of the project. In most large contracts, a different billing and payment schedule is agreed upon.

PERCENT OF PHASE COMPLETED

As with any of the management techniques that we have discussed thus far, our philosophy is that any project, regardless of how large, should be broken down into easily understandable parts. The project should be divided into the same phases as time accounting, cost estimating, and job costing. Each phase will thus represent a given percentage of the overall project. This method of billing is generally referred to as percentage of phase completed.

In a sample flat fee contract of $100,000 each phase would have a given value. For example let us assume the phases are as follows:

PROFESSIONAL FEES PER
CONTRACT DATED 10/27/84 $100,000.00

Phase	% of Contract	% Completed	Total
Schematic Design	20%	0	0
Design Development	30%	0	0
Construction Documents	30%	0	0
Contract Administration	20%	0	0
Total	100%		0

Therefore those phases that are 20 percent of the overall contract are worth $20,000 and phases that are 30 percent of the overall contract are worth $30,000.

One mistake that many firms make is that they do not begin to fill in the matrix until a phase is 100 percent complete and thus send the client a bill only for reimbursable expenses in the interim. This method of billing has several obvious and not so obvious problems.

1. Naturally your cash flow is hurt since the expenses of performing the professional services continue on a week-by-week and month-by-month basis, yet the first income from the project may not come in until months after the work is begun. Even then, remember that most clients of A/E firms do not write a check and send a runner to your office when the bill arrives in the mail.
2. We have known firms that were so desperate for money by the time that the phase was ready to be billed that the owners themselves went to the client's office to present the bill and attempted to collect a check immediately. You can readily see that this is not the best way to run a professional business.
3. As a corollary to (2), this method of billing requires that your staff prepare bills at odd times and cycles during the month.

It precludes all of the efficiency that we are trying to encourage. We have found that the support staff who prepare the bill are given precious little time to do the job and do it right.
4. The credit worthiness of some clients of A/E firms may be questionable. If all of your clients are the U.S. government or other good credit risks, this may not apply. In this method of billing, you do not send periodic bills and thus cannot automatically measure the client's ability and intention to pay until a large receivable is incurred. If this possibly represents a large percentage of the income for your firm for a given period, their failure to pay promptly or at all can cause unbelievable hardship to your firm. We have seen firms almost sink when this happens on a large project. Sending smaller invoices as the work progresses provides you with more assurances and, in the long run, better benefits the client.
5. In the event of disagreements, money up front as the project progresses provides you with a subtle or stated degree of leverage.

We could go on and on belaboring the obvious: An invoice should be sent to the client each and every month on a set schedule. The professional services should be billed as a percentage of each phase completed at the cutoff date of the invoice. We also feel that if a second phase is started and substantial professional services have been performed on that phase, even though a previous phase is not 100 percent complete, both phases should be billed. The matrix for the invoice should look something like the following:

PROFESSIONAL FEES PER
CONTRACT DATED 10/27/84 $100,000.00

Phase	% of Contract	% Completed	Total
Schematic Design	20%	90%	18,000
Design Development	30%	10%	3,000
Construction Documents	30%	0%	0
Contract Administration	20%	0%	0
Total	100%		21,000
Less Paid To Date	15,000		
Total Due	**6,000**		

Further informational refinements may be made by subtracting the amount past due from the total due in order to indicate the amount of new money being billed in a particular month.

Billing therefore becomes a routine monthly procedure of filling in the matrix, increasing the various phases involved as to the percentage completed, and performing the related math required.

PERCENTAGE OF CONSTRUCTION COST

Another variation of the flat fee is the percentage of construction cost. At one time this was an extremely popular method of writing contracts. It is still in use by many firms, especially those that do governmental or institutional projects. If you are an engineer and are a consultant to an architect who has entered into this type of contract, the architect may insist that your fee be based on the percentage of construction cost so that he may control the engineering consulting costs as a percentage of the fee he will receive.

This type of contract has some good points and some bad points. The good points are directly dependent on how large the percentage of the construction cost is. For an architect there are no benefits in a contract written as 0.5 percent of construction cost. At the same time there is nothing wrong with a contract written at 50 percent of construction costs. Therefore this discussion will make the assumption that the original percentage fee agreed upon is reasonable.

Reasonable means that the initial contract meets all the criteria of a flat fee contract if the final dollars were treated as such in the cost estimation formulas previously discussed. If the construction costs are at least the initial estimate, then the contract is a good one.

The fundamental premise of the percentage of construction cost contract is that if the construction costs increase it is because the scope of the contract and the professional services of the A/E firm have also increased in the same proportion and, therefore, the firm is entitled to additional compensation. On the other hand, if the construction costs are lower than the initial estimate, it is because the scope of the contract and the professional services of the A/E firm have also decreased and therefore the firm is entitled to less compensation.

Although there may be some theoretical validity to this, it assumes that you were perfect when you made your original estimate concerning the final construction costs. One of the biggest drawbacks, besides the obvious monetary problems, is that if the construction costs are way off, one side or the other is going to feel cheated. This is especially true if the reason for the additional construction costs is not directly related to additional requirements of the client.

Keeping all the above caveats in mind, let us see how this type of contract is billed and review the accounting method that should be used.

First the actual contract is computed to an actual dollar amount for the professional fees, based on an initial estimate of the construction costs. The project should then be divided into phases, as in the percentage of phase completed method. Until such time as the estimate of the construction cost is changed or updated, the project is treated exactly as the percentage of phase completed.

ESTIMATED CONSTRUCTION COST
$2,000,000 PERCENTAGE FEE 5%
PROFESSIONAL FEES PER
CONTRACT DATED 10/27/84 $100,000

Phase	% of Contract	% Completed	Total
Schematic Design	20%	90%	18,000
Design Development	30%	10%	3,000
Construction Documents	30%	0%	0
Contract Administration	20%	0%	0
Total	100%		21,000
Less Paid To Date	15,000		
Total Due	**6,000**		

The above use of 5 percent is simply to make the contract amount equal to the previous example of $100,000 and is in no way a recommendation that this should be the percentage fee charged.

Once the fee is determined, the contract and billing procedures are treated in a manner similar to a flat fee based on percentage of phase completed. The difference between the percentage of phase completed contract and the percentage of construction cost contract comes when the estimate of the construction costs is changed and the timing of when the change should be made. Thus, the flat fee of the percentage of construction cost contract can change with each monthly billing to the client.

Once you know that the construction costs are going to differ from the original estimate or even the last estimate, you should periodically update them. There should also be an automatic recalculation of the amount due. What this means is that the client will immediately owe an additional amount on the already completed work since each of the percentages that have been billed are multiplied by higher construction costs. In this way the client is paying the increase on a periodic basis. We know of firms that wait until the end of the project, when all costs of construction are absolutely known, and then present the client with an additional invoice for $20,000 or more. This can be quite a shock to a client and we have seen cases where such an unexpected amount was difficult to collect.

SQUARE FEET

Billing by the square foot is a method often used by design firms. It is essentially the same as the flat fee methods described above, except it is more of a combination of the two. The format of the square foot method is very similar to the percentage of construction cost except that any increase in the final contract is more directly related to a change in the scope of the project since in order to change the final contract, the square feet constructed or designed or space planned increase or decrease.

ESTIMATED SQUARE FEET
50,000 SQUARE FOOT COST $2.00
PROFESSIONAL FEES PER
CONTRACT DATED 10/27/84 $100,000

Phase	% of Contract	% Completed	Total
Schematic Design	20%	90%	18,000
Design Development	30%	10%	3,000
Construction Documents	30%	0%	0
Contract Administration	20%	0%	0
Total	100%		21,000
Less Paid To Date	15,000		
Total Due	**6,000**		

Here again, the use of $2 per square foot is simply to make the contract amount equal to the previous examples of $100,000 and is in no way a recommendation that this should be the amount per square foot charged.

HYBRIDS

One of the most common billing methods, and the most complicated to account for, is the hybrid method. This can be used with any of the above flat fee methods, with additional services billed on an hourly basis.

The reason this is so complicated is that it must be controlled and accounted for at three points in the billing cycle:

1. At the point of the time sheet, someone must make a decision whether the hours that are being worked are for the contract portion of the project or the additional services portion of the project. This is generally communicated along the line to the support staff that will actually prepare the bill.
2. When the bill is prepared, the percentage completed must be kept separate from the additional hourly services since the total amount paid on the contract is subtracted from the flat fee portion of the bill.
3. In order to facilitate (2), accounts receivable must at all times maintain a record of the amount owed on the contract (flat fee) and on all the noncontract items such as the additional hourly services, as well as reimbursable charges. When the client makes a payment, it must be distributed in a dual manner.

If you are using a computer for your billings, be certain that your program has this feature; your only alternative is to set up two bills and send the additional services out as a completely separate invoice. This is a workable solution but most A/E firms prefer to combine the contract on one bill unless the additional service is extremely large. You should not have to change such a common way of doing business to accommodate a computer program.

Accounts Payable

One of the essential elements of good management is the proper allocation of expenditures with their corresponding revenues. The IRS recognizes two methods of accounting: cash basis and accrual basis. If your firm wishes to remain on a cash basis for IRS tax reporting, that is perfectly alright and is up to you and your accountant. But for management purposes, cash accounting is one step below useless.

Let us first define what we mean by accrual accounting for management purposes. We are not really interested in absolute accruals, which your accountant may insist on. Our purpose here is to generally match expenditures with their corresponding revenues. When money is received (on the receivables side) and when money is actually expended (on the accounts payable side) has no relationship to the monthly earnings of a company.

For example, your company might have many large receivables sustaining your cash flow on a monthly basis. A cash basis accounting system would show that the company is doing well when in actuality you might be losing money each month and not knowing it. Conversely large receivables each month may be putting a cash flow crunch on the business, but the company is doing very well in its business and expansion. The point is that you must use accrual accounting even in a very limited format to be able to get any kind of meaningful information from your income statement and from your general ledger.

Without getting bogged down in a long bookkeeping lesson, let us look at the entries used when working with accounts payable.

First we should set up some imaginary accounts. Assume 1111 is cash, 2112 is accounts payable, and 6111 is any expenditure account.

When expenditures are actually made, meaning when the invoice comes into the office, the following entry is made:

ACCOUNT		DEBIT	CREDIT
6111	Expenditure Account	500	
2112	Accounts Payable		500

Since no cash is actually leaving the company, the accounts payable account is credited instead of the cash account. The expenditure is made as a debit to the expenditure account even though the bill has not been paid. In this way the expenditures are posted in the month in which they occur regardless of when the check is actually written.

Let us say that for several months the company has been in a very cash-poor position and has not paid any of its bills. The expenditures that have been accumulating during this time have been properly posted to their proper expenditure accounts even though no checks except payroll have been written. Therefore the monthly income statements represent close to the actual profit/loss for each month, although some adjustments might have to be made to the general ledger for absolute accuracy. Several months later, we receive a large receivable check, which permits us to pay all of our bills in one month. The following entry would be made:

ACCOUNT		DEBIT	CREDIT
2112	Accounts Payable	20,000	
1111	Cash		20,000

Notice that the expenditure of all that cash in one month had absolutely no effect on the income statement for that month since the debit was to accounts payable and not to an expenditure account.

This is the general theory of accounts payable and is not difficult to understand. For even a moderate-size firm, however, this can become very cumbersome because of the amount of manual bookkeeping involved. A good computer system can make this laborious task extremely easy and can actually write the checks for you. It can also keep track of how much has been expended for each of your vendors.

The following are some of the things you should look for in good computer accounts payable programs:

1. The most difficult thing to work with in any accounts payable program is the numbering of the vendors in order to keep them in alphabetical order. The computer should be able to keep track of this task for you; otherwise, you could be

spending an enormous amount of time keeping vendors in the right numerical and alphabetical order.

2. The program should give you a complete history of all open *and* closed invoices for all vendors.
3. You should be permitted to pay any, all, or part of any invoice.
4. There should be total and absolute integration with the corresponding general ledger program.
5. The program should be date-sensitive and be able to provide you with cash flow projections.
6. You should be able to age the payments of the payables, thus paying the earliest ones first.

The use of accounts payable should not become overly difficult or involved. Just remember that your main purpose is to allocate the expenditures into their proper months so that you can properly manage the income and expenditures of your company and receive some meaningful and timely information.

Work in Progress

The ideal managerial approach, and the basis of accrual accounting for management, is to be able to properly allocate revenue to its corresponding expenses for the same time period. It tells you little that revenue for one month was over expenses for another. Although this profit/loss statement over a period of time will even out, it does not give you the management information necessary to properly judge the efficiency and profitability of the organization in a timely manner.

If your bills, payroll, and time sheets are all calculated on the last day of the month, this discussion is academic because each of these items and your general ledger are all cutting off at the same time. Therefore there is no timing problem.

But unfortunately the last day of the month is the worst time to finish anything except the general ledger. As we discussed in billing, if your cutoff is the last day of the month, your bills will not go out until after the 1st. Many times you will miss client deadlines for payment and thus aged receivables will lag.

The last day of the month is often an impractical payroll date for many firms. This is because it places an undue burden on those who prepare the payroll to produce a paycheck before the time sheet is in. If you are currently paying on the 15th and last day, then a change to the 1st and 16th, with cutoffs on the 15th and 31st, will greatly enhance the timeliness of your reports.

Let us assume for the moment that your cutoff date for billing is the 21st of each month. This means that your billing period is from the 22nd of one month through the 21st of another. Therefore your invoices, which are booked in receivables for the current month, include work performed during the eight or nine days of the previous month and are missing eight or nine days of the current month.

Naturally if the amount of work performed in each of these periods is the same and represents approximately the same billing, there is no problem. But, if you are doing the same thing each and every month, you have no management problems. What you have is a money machine.

Your work in progress is the net difference between the ending days of the previous month and the ending days of the current month.

Once this figure is known, it is very easy to make an adjustment in the general ledger.

Debit: work in progress (receivables account)
Credit: work in progress (revenue account)

Many firms call these accounts unbilled services. As with the receivables adjustment, you may either post the difference or back out the old and post the new in its entirety.

Securing the work in progress figure is a little tricky without a computer. It should be done through time accounting. If you have nothing but hourly projects, it is an easy process to calculate by hand or do a search on the computer for the amounts billed for the two time periods. Actually you will need to calculate only one time period since you already have the information from the previous one.

The complication comes with the flat fee projects that do not secure their revenue on an hourly basis. Figuring what percentage was completed on each project for two eight- or nine-day periods is an almost impossible task. Through time accounting, however, you do know the hours performed and the billing rates per person that would have been charged if the project had been hourly. If you have a computer, the billing rate should be posted as an hourly project, with the billing flag set for "No" for billing purposes. This should allow you to report on an hourly billing basis and still bill by flat fee. Your time accounting program will have to be able to make this distinction.

Through this procedure, securing the information for work in progress can be obtained in a matter of minutes with the proper computer program. Following these simple procedures will assure that your general ledger becomes a much better management tool for many purposes.

Payroll

Payroll is made complicated because of the myriad of rules and regulations imposed by various regulatory agencies. Because regulations tend to differ from state to state, we will confine our discussion here to federal regulations and general state unemployment reporting requirements. We will also include a section on the effect of payroll expenditures on other seemingly unrelated business expenditures. And we will attempt to analyze the general cost of payroll dollars to the employer and suggest ways to minimize the impact.

Frequency of payroll is always an important decision. The IRS recognizes several standard payroll periods:

Weekly	One time per week
Biweekly	Every other week
Bimonthly	Twice per month
Monthly	One time per month

Naturally many factors must be taken into consideration when determining the best payroll period for each firm. In some cases state law will decide whether the monthly payroll period is legal. Also, many of your employees may have a difficult time budgeting their own finances if paid only once a month. On the other hand, the monthly payroll form is the best for cash flow of the firm.

Biweekly and bimonthly payrolls are functionally the same for the general cash flow of the firm. The obvious difference is that there are 26 pay periods with the biweekly form and 24 pay periods for the bimonthly form. But the biggest consideration will be in coordinating the payroll with the time sheet cycle and reports. It is absolutely imperative that the payroll be coordinated with the time sheets.

One other consideration is when the payroll is actually prepared. Many firms try to actually produce the payroll checks before the time sheets are turned in to the business office. For example, the 1st and the 15th are very popular pay dates. Many times checks will be produced and in the hands of the employees before 2:00 P.M. on the 15th for time as of 5:00 P.M. that day. This creates an impossible situation for the individuals who have to prepare the payroll. Creating a cutoff date for time sheets at least one day prior to the actual payroll will help immensely.

Many employers consider federal taxes, which are withheld from the employees' paychecks, to be a burden to the cash flow of the firm. In a cash-poor firm the amount necessary to meet the payroll by payday is often computed as the overall net. Unfortunately the IRS has other ideas concerning monies that are withheld from the employees' paychecks. In fact the IRS's concern that you do not begin to consider it your money is so great that they have issued regulations which require that if the amount owed to Uncle Sam exceeds certain amounts you must deposit the money in a federal depository (most banks) by the end of the banking day on the third business day following the date of the payroll. Failure to do this results in a penalty by the IRS called failure to make timely deposits. It can be very costly. For more information, consult the IRS booklet currently referred to as Circular E. These deposit regulations are also part of the instructions for the 941 form. The important thing to remember is that there are three break points which determine when the federal deposit is to be made. The dollar amount will differ depending on the regulations in effect at any given time. These dollar amounts refer to how much money is owed at any point in time.

1. By three banking days after payroll date
2. By the 15th of the following month
3. By the 15th of the month after the quarter ends

Be very careful. Even though the amount due the IRS traditionally puts you in the second category, you could still become a three-day depositor by issuing a bonus payroll during the month. It is not enough to pay just the amount due to return to the monthly depositor category. Once you become a three-day depositor, all monies owed the IRS are due within three days of the last payroll. The IRS is extremely good at catching this error and enforcing this penalty. It provides a substantial amount of income for the IRS and at the same time ensures that the cash flow to the IRS will not be unduly delayed to the advantage of the employer.

Let us now look at the taxes that must be withheld from an employee's paycheck by the employer. The first, and many times the largest amount, is federal withholding. This is the income tax withheld from paychecks. If you are computing this manually, you should be familiar with the IRS Circular E booklet. You simply find the appropriate number of exemptions in the married or single table and the amount of the gross; the table will tell you how much to withhold from the check. Generally most computer programs will produce this automatically.

The next biggest bite is FICA tax. This is the Social Security contribution made by both the employer and the employee. It is generally computed as an absolute percentage of the gross up to what is known as the FICA limit. Both the FICA limit and the percentage amounts can be found in various IRS publications. Once the FICA limit has been reached, no more FICA tax is to be deducted from the employee's paychecks. This is trickier than it sounds. Most of the time the FICA limit is reached in the middle of a payroll. For example, if an employee makes $1000 per pay period and needs only $200 more to reach the FICA limit, the first $200 of the payroll is taxed and the balance of the $800 is "free" on the same payroll. Generally, however, the FICA limit is set so high that only a few employees within a firm ever reach it.

The employer also pays a matching FICA tax. Actually the burden of the FICA tax is totally on the employer, as will be seen in the actual computation of the 941 report. Let us assume that the FICA tax and the matching employer FICA tax are 7.15 percent each. When you are filling out the 941 report, you will notice that there is no reference to the amount that is withheld from the employee. The employer simply pays 14.3 percent of the total gross for all payrolls during the period. If the employer has withheld enough from the employees, the employer is covered. If the employer has not withheld enough, the employer in actuality is paying the FICA for the employee. This is probably alright in minor instances. The IRS, however, takes a dim view of this practice if it becomes a standard procedure. The employer is required to report as income to the employee on his W2 at the end of the year the amount of FICA tax paid by the employer.

These are the two federal taxes that we are most familiar with. There are some miscellaneous state taxes, which may include state income tax, state unemployment tax, and so on. Check with your state to determine exactly what its requirements are.

In addition to state taxes, there are other items that may be withheld from an employee's paycheck. These items are generally referred to as deductions. They reflect money that the employee owes to the employer or vice versa. What is important to note concerning these deductions is that they are deducted from after-tax income or net. They are not deducted from the gross, that is, before FICA and federal withholding taxes are computed. Therefore they have no effect whatsoever on the total gross that will appear at the end of the year on the W2 of the employee.

These deductions, of course, will vary but may be for such things as health care, dental insurance, parking, and advances. The employer may even be giving money back to the employee for such things as out-of-pocket expenses, mileage, or other reimbursements. These work in much the same way as other deductions but are negative deductions. Remember that they are added to or subtracted from the after-tax income and are thus made neutral insofar as the gross pay of the employee is concerned.

One of the items mentioned above was the advance. This is a particularly difficult problem for many employers to handle, though in reality it is quite easy. When an employee needs an advance or an early paycheck, the check is written as any other check to a vendor in the general ledger. The general ledger entry is a credit to cash and a debit to employee receivables. At this point the check that was written is not a payroll check as far as the general ledger is concerned. It is just another check to a vendor. When the next payroll period arrives, the employee receives the full amount of his gross check. All taxes, withholding, FICA, and so on, are computed on the full gross. A miscellaneous deduction is made to the after-tax net for the amount of the advance. Therefore the net received by the employee is his regular paycheck less the amount of the advance. As you will see later in the discussion of payroll distribution to the general ledger, this deduction will be spread back to the employee receivables account to close it out and pay off the receivable due from the employee.

Every dollar amount written from payroll must eventually be distributed to the general ledger. Payroll makes up the single largest expenditure of most firms. Therefore it should always be properly distributed to the correct general ledger direct and indirect accounts. Failure to make the proper distribution will highly skew all of the items that are affected by direct or indirect expenditures.

Time accounting will help greatly by giving you the information for any given pay period on the direct and indirect hours worked for each of the employees. Let us emphasize again that this is critical. The difficulty lies in the vast differences in how the gross for employees is computed.

The gross for employees who are straight hourly is easy to compute because time accounting will give you the number of hours and these hours may be plugged directly into the payroll system as direct or indirect hours.

Employees who are salaried present a slightly different situation. The number of hours worked is incidental to the amount of gross pay that they are to receive. But what we are interested in here is how much of that constant dollar amount is to be allocated to direct and how much to indirect general ledger accounts. This is done simply as a ratio. If an employee's gross is $1,000 as straight salary and his direct hours are 40 percent of the total hours, you simply apply $400 to the direct general ledger account and $600 to the indirect account.

Overtime presents still another unique problem: exactly which hours are overtime and which straight time. This is an absolutely impossible task. Even if you decided that those hours spent after 5:00 P.M. are overtime and all others are straight time, and meticulously kept track of what the employee was doing during the overtime hours, you would still not have accomplished your goal. Who is to say that working till 7:00 P.M. on a project that had to go out by 5:00 P.M. did not cause two hours of indirect overtime? In actuality, in this simple case it would be fairer to apply the two hours of overtime to direct instead of indirect because the overtime was the result of the project-related deadline. An unlimited number of scenarios could be conjured up that would drive any manager insane.

We feel that the important thing is consistency. Where overtime is concerned, we recommend that if the employee works on projects, then all overtime should be applied to direct general ledger accounts. If, on the other hand, the employee does not work on projects, then all overtime should be applied to the indirect general ledger accounts. Such consistency prevents any skewing of the ratios.

Remember, in the general ledger each employee group should have at least two accounts: direct payroll and indirect payroll. For example, salaries of the principals (both direct and indirect) might be one group and employee salaries (both direct and indirect) another. If you departmentalize there may be more, but they will all follow the same pattern of direct and indirect.

The spreading of payroll and its variations to the general ledger is not an easy task. The following shows only one of many ways that it might be done. We have chosen this method because of its simplicity and because it gives you the ability to easily balance and cross-check if anything has been done improperly.

First it is important to note that neither the IRS nor any other regulatory agency requires that you report FICA and federal withholding separately on your general ledger. This is required only on each employee's W2. Any good payroll program will handle this function for you automatically. Therefore we recommend that you simply have a single clearing account for both FICA and withholding in your general ledger, in the liabilities section of accounts. Let us call this Federal 941 Withholding, account number 2141.

The next account you will need will be a clearing account for all miscellaneous deductions. By doing this you will not have to worry about the general ledger spread for every deduction for every employee at the time you are doing the payroll. We will call this Deductions Payable, account number 2142.

You may or may not need to have a state withholding account. If you do, you can call it State Tax Payable, account number 2143. As stated previously these are all examples and may be named or numbered differently. They should, of course, all be placed in the liability section of your general ledger.

Let us assume that the totals to your check register for payroll are as follows:

GROSS	WITHHOLDING	FICA	DEDUCTIONS	NET
5000	800	350	100	3750

The following entries would be made to the general ledger:

ACCOUNT		DEBIT	CREDIT
6111	Indirect Gross	3000	
6112	Direct Gross	2000	
2141	Federal 941 Payable		1150
2142	Deductions Payable		100
1111	Cash		3750

Notice that the debits do equal the credits. The total amount of the gross is spread between the indirect and the direct general ledger accounts. In actual practice, this could be several accounts, but two should be the minimum. The FICA and the federal withholding are added together and posted as a credit to the Federal 941 Payable account. Note that there was no attempt to separate them out since the 941 report does not require that you do so. All other deductions are posted as a credit to the Deductions Payable account. The net amount of the payroll is posted as a credit to cash because this is the actual amount of money that left your bank account at this time. Let us reemphasize that gross is posted to the direct and indirect general ledger expenditure accounts, and net is posted to cash. This is where most mistakes occur.

Remember that the above payable accounts are clearing accounts. They are not intended to be a permanent collection of the amount of monies withheld from each of the employees. Therefore, ideally before each payroll the clearing accounts should clear out to zero. Let us take the Federal 941 account as an example. So far you have deposited a credit which represents the sum of the FICA and the federal withholding to that account. You will shortly be expected to write a check to the IRS or to your federal depository for an amount equal to what you have credited to this account plus an amount of matching FICA. You may debit 2141 for $1150 and split the rest of the debit to your matching FICA expense account. Therefore when you write a check to the IRS or the federal depository, the clearing account 2141 will return to zero. In this way, you can be sure you are always current with tax deposits. If you ever fail to pay your 941 money, there will be a balance in 2141. This is extremely easy to balance even if you are not a three-day depositor since the total in this account represents the amount of FICA and withholding from each of the payrolls.

An alternative method would be to immediately make a journal entry as a debit to the matching FICA expense account and a credit to 2141 for the amount of the matching FICA. This would place into the 2141 account the total obligation due to the IRS. When you wrote your check you would be debiting from 2141 for the entire amount rather than split-coding it. Also the balance of this account would represent a single cumulative amount, which could be tracked and which would warn you if you were approaching one of the break points that could throw you into the three-day depositor category.

The miscellaneous deduction account is handled in a similar manner. Remember that *everything* in this account belongs somewhere else. Therefore each large group, such as health insurance, should be debited from the 2142 account and credited to an appropriate insurance expenditure account. The same will occur for advances, parking, and so on. Ideally, all of the clearing accounts in the example—2141, 2142, and 2143—should be cleared out to zero before you begin your next payroll.

Some good payroll programs have the ability to handle personnel reports as well as leave reports. The information you should expect from even a rudimentary personnel report would include the name, address, telephone number, and other general directory information on all of your employees. Financial information would include yearly salary, hourly salary (whether or not paid hourly), date of employment, date of last raise, billing rate, and the like. This is information that managers should have at their fingertips.

Leave information is not really that complicated to keep track of on a computer payroll program. It should be handled either on a day or half day basis or by the hour. Some firms have a policy that each employee is to accumulate various types of leave at so many hours per month. It is therefore necessary for the payroll program to be able to accrue leave based on the policies of the company. The deduction of leave from the balances of each employee should also be handled by the payroll program.

It is essential that a payroll program be able to handle one type of leave for an A/E firm. This is compensatory time. Many firms offer comp time in lieu of overtime for employees. Over the years we have seen some very interesting policies. Some have bordered on the absurd. For example, it does no one any good to offer comp time to a strictly hourly employee, especially one who is paid time and a half for overtime. We know of several firms that have had this policy. In one, the employees quickly learned that if they accumulated comp time they could use that time to boost normal nonovertime hours into overtime. The important thing to note is that comp time is a very valued benefit for mainly salaried employees who put in time in excess of regular working hours. It is essential that large amounts of comp time not be permitted to build up. If they do, you should check the laws of your state to see if you have to pay the then-existing hourly rate for any accumulated comp time for a departing employee.

Our advice is that if you use comp time be sure to use it for what it was intended and make sure that it is taken by your employees as soon as possible.

Finally let us turn our discussion to the cost of payroll as opposed to other expenditures. Every expenditure reduces net profit. Of course we would prefer to have only revenue and no expenditures. Unfortunately that is not the way it works. But not all expenditures are created equal. Some are taxed for the mere privilege of making those expenditures. Payroll is one of those items.

Unlike an expenditure for computer supplies, we pay various taxes, directly and indirectly, for every dollar that is classified as a payroll expenditure. The most obvious of these taxes is the matching FICA tax, which averages in excess of 7 percent and is scheduled to increase each year. FUTA is a federal unemployment tax that is often overlooked until the end of the year, when you are shocked to find that you owe a penalty for not making timely deposits. FUTA averages a little under 1 percent of the payroll cost up to a FUTA limit, which now is very low. There may be other state taxes that are taxed directly to the employer based on the gross amount of the payroll.

The above are the direct taxes to payroll. There are other incidental costs that are directly or indirectly affected by the size of the payroll expenditures. They include such items as workmen's compensation insurance. This may run you anywhere from less than 1 percent of the payroll to a whopping 7 to 8 percent of an employee's gross pay. Liability insurance for many companies is based on the amount of the company's payroll. The point here is not that you should avoid paying your taxes or insurance, but that you become aware of the actual cost of each payroll dollar that you expend.

Shifting some of the payroll expenditures from payroll to other ordinary expenditures would greatly enhance the bottom line of the company by not subjecting those expenditures to these high costs. We have estimated that each payroll dollar costs the average employer 12 to 15 percent of the gross salaries paid. Let us mention here one method commonly used to shift payroll expenditures to nonpayroll expenditures. That is the use of contract labor, which is loosely defined as individuals hired for a specific short-term project. Keep in mind, however, that there are strict regulations concerning who may be classified as contract labor and who is considered an employee, and the penalties imposed at both the state and the federal levels if you are caught trying to defraud the government by claiming employees as contract labor instead of employees are severe. Check with your attorney or accountant. This is not a technique that we recommend. It could be very costly to you both in the short run and in the long run.

One of the best legal ways to shift discretionary salary monies into ordinary expenditures is to do so with the salaries of the owners of the firm. If your business is a sole proprietorship or a partnership, there is not much that can be done. You cannot pay yourself a salary anyway. And the amount of money that you make is subject to self-employment tax, which is almost equal to the FICA and the matching FICA combined. In addition you are not usually covered by workmen's compensation, which you might not consider until you read the fine print in your company's health insurance clause that says that the insurance will pay for on-the-job injuries only after workmen's compensation pays what is legally required by law. You might be shocked to learn that you are the only employee in the company not covered by workmen's compensation and thus not insured for on-the-job injuries. Naturally this will depend on the health insurance policy that your company has.

It is our belief that a Sub Chapter S Corporation is one of the best vehicles for any small organization to have. Through this type of corporate organization you have the discretion of how much salary you pay the owners and thus how much salary tax you pay on that salary. At the same time all income from the corporation is taxed to the individual owners directly on their own 1040s. Thus you do not have the double taxation that is present in a standard corporation. Consult your attorney and accountant for details.

Other methods of shifting salary expenditures to nonsalary expenditures involve benefits, although the IRS is now disallowing many of these. Health and life insurance is one that is still a nontaxable benefit to the employee and a deductible nonpayroll expenditure to the employer. Be sure to get professional advice concerning appropriate state and federal regulations before you embark on this course.

Conclusion

Project management and financial accounting are not part-time jobs. A/E firms have unique financial and accounting problems that are not encountered by other industries. The only thing A/E firms have to sell is their expertise and creativity translated into *time.* The need to integrate time accounting and financial accounting into one managerial system is what makes the A/E firm unique.

It is easy to make money during good times. If you are a good architect or engineer and have good people on your team and if the fees in your area are high, you do not have to practice good business principles. You can afford to be sloppy in your bidding, spend money on things that do not increase productivity, and worry about the bookkeeping later.

As we all know, however, good times do not last forever. When a recession hits, whether it is a local building recession or a national one, the weak firms suffer more than the strong ones do. Unfortunately firms in a bad market begin to learn project management and financial accounting out of desperation and a crying need.

Although we have tried in this section to touch on what we consider to be the major principles of good project management and financial accounting, we have not covered everything. And keep in mind that it takes many months to begin to incorporate everything we have covered here into a working system customized to the needs of your firm. Even if you do not do everything we have outlined here, do something. You must begin. Haphazard project management and financial accounting will undercut profits and possibly lead to disaster. Neither small firms nor large ones are exempt.

There is an investment involved. This may be monetary or it may be in effort and time. But there is a difference between a cost and an investment. In any investment you anticipate receiving something that is greater than the initial investment. If you invest a little time and money in following the procedures outlined here and establish good project management and financial accounting techniques, you will have the necessary tools to handle most situations.

What about the computer? Will it save you money? That is the wrong question. The question should be, Will it *make* you money? In other words, Is it an investment or a cost? That depends on what you are going to use it for. Here the right software is critical because without it a computer is one of the most expensive paperweights you have ever owned.

If you are buying a computer simply for its word processing capabilities and you are heavy into specifications, then it can be justified as an expensive and efficient typewriter. If you add marketing through mailouts and mailing lists, you are starting to approach a return on the investment. Add bookkeeping to this and you are providing for information processing, which can give you management information, which can begin to keep your company on track. Add complete project management and financial accounting specifically for A/E firms and the answer to cost versus investment becomes obvious.

When you consider the low cost of computer systems in today's market, it is obvious that manual operations cannot begin to compete. Not only is it more economical to provide information from a microcomputer, but also the information is more accurate and is always timely. After deducting IRS participation in its purchase and spreading the cost over the five years the IRS provides, the cost of a complete computer system is usually not much more than $100 per month. The question you must answer is, Can a system as we have outlined it here make you more than $100 per month? We know it can!

PART 2

HOW TO MARKET A/E SERVICES

Introduction

We have found throughout our years of working with A/E firms that there is a reluctance on the part of these companies to do any marketing whatsoever. Many professionals resist marketing because they see it as an attempt to change a profession into a retail outlet. There is also the factor of professional ethics. Public advertising or marketing has been permitted only recently by many professions, and architects and engineers have followed these guidelines in the past.

The ideas and concepts that will be discussed in this section are meant to provide the professional architect or engineer with methods of organizing and conducting professional marketing strategies that will provide a continuous stream of business. Not all concepts contained here should be applied at the same time. We earnestly believe that the best marketing strategy is to begin adopting, little by little, those concepts that you feel comfortable with and, for the present, dismissing those that are uncomfortable for you. What is important is to *begin*.

Unfortunately the saying "If you build a better mousetrap the world will beat a path to your door" is untrue. How good your mousetrap is has absolutely nothing whatsoever to do, in the short run, with whether or not you can sell it. This is not to say that if you continually produce a shoddy product or service your business can succeed. But even though your business or service is the absolute best in the community, if nobody knows about it, you will not be in business for very long. That is exactly what marketing is: telling others about what you do. The term *marketing* is used to encompass four areas: advertising, public relations, market analysis, and selling.

We have found that what most architects and engineers call marketing is what we call "buttonholing." Although this is a valid form of marketing, and we have included substantial material regarding this concept, it is by far the least productive of all marketing strategies. Basically buttonholing consists of community activities and social get-togethers where you attempt to meet individuals who might be able to do you some good. The problem with this type of marketing strategy is that all other architects and engineers in your community are doing the same thing, meeting the same people, and attending the same meetings. The sad truth of it is that there is no way, considering the time limitations of a twenty-four hour day, that you can attend enough meetings or meet enough people to produce the numbers necessary for you to be the architect or engineer on a developer's mind when his project is ready. This method of marketing is so popular only because:

1. It is easy.
2. It is nonthreatening.
3. It has all the earmarks of professionalism.
4. It deludes you into believing that you are spending your time effectively marketing for your company.

There is nothing wrong with buttonholing if it is not the *only* strategy used by your company.

What we will try to do in this section is to give you the tools to organize your marketing strategies so you can begin doing something. The worlds of architecture and engineering are becoming more and more competitive, and it will be those who have consistent marketing strategies as well as good professional services who are going to succeed.

Is This You?

We would like you to first take a short test, which consists of statements and questions concerning attitudes we have found to be pervasive throughout the industry. As you read them and identify the particular concepts with the emphasis your firm puts on each one, you will be able to then get an informal picture of exactly what activities your firm is engaged in, what you consider marketing to be, and where your marketing resources and dollars are going.

There are no right or wrong answers to this test. It is intended only to provide you with a picture of yourself so that you can see where you are coming from, help point out where you are heading, and identify when you have arrived.

I am not a salesman.

First let us point out that even though you are architects and engineers, if you own your firm, you are in the business of selling. There are no professions or businesses, outside of government, that do not have to sell something in order to survive. Even the telephone company now has to sell. We live in a capitalistic society, which means that you are in competition with people who do the same thing you do. It is not enough simply to produce and engage in business activities. You must make a profit if you are to survive in this society. The only way to make a profit is to sell something to someone for less money than it cost you to produce it. Regardless of what you wish to call it—providing a service, consulting, professional services—the client is purchasing something from you. As long as that client has a choice, it is your job to convince him that your service is in his best interest. This is selling.

Are you still a victim of the myth of the "born salesman"? It *is* a myth. There is no such thing as a born salesman. Salesmen *learn* to sell.

There are methods of moving clients off dead center and getting them to say yes. These techniques are learned and acquired, not inherited. There is no easy way. You must learn selling techniques; you must use selling techniques; and you must constantly practice selling techniques. The day you become aware that you *are* a salesman, regardless of how you wish to disguise it, will be the day that you sell more. Simply stated, this is when you get your clients to become aware that your services are in their best interest and that they should proceed with the project using your A/E firm.

Advertising is wrong.

To many individuals within the A/E environment, the word *advertising* is repulsive, and we have even known firms that refused to use the word, even on their general ledger. Advertising is simply that part of marketing that lets your clients know that you exist and can provide the services necessary for them to proceed with their project. It lets them know what you can do for them. You, of course, are going to have to make a decision on what type of advertising you are going to undertake. The only wrong advertising is ineffective advertising. For example, you could take out a television ad with a used-car type of salesman holding up a set of blueprints while announcing a two-for-one sale on schematic designs. We are, of course, being facetious in our example, but the reason this advertising is wrong is not necessarily because it is in and of itself sleazy, unprofessional, and in poor taste. What really makes it wrong is that it will not work because others *perceive* it as being sleazy, unprofessional, and in poor taste. On the other hand, this type of advertising works very well for the used-car salesman because it is expected of him. Advertising is neither right nor wrong; rather, it either works or it does not. It is your job to discover the advertising technique that will be most effective for your firm.

Are you afraid to pick up the telephone?

No, we are not talking about answering the phone when it rings. No, we are not talking about returning a client's call or answering an inquiry. What we are talking about is picking up the phone and calling to tell someone about yourself and what you do. We are not suggesting at this time that you pick up the phone and do cold-calling to every business in the *Yellow Pages* to offer a special deal on schematics this month. Remember, this is not effective. First you must identify for yourself whether or not you have telephone phobia. In a chapter that follows, we *are* going to recommend that you call a qualified potential client and ask to meet him. We have never known of a successful architectural or engineering firm that has provided services to a client on a regular basis without meeting him. Except perhaps in rare situations, there is no way that you are going to successfully sell the client on your services until you first meet him. If you do have telephone phobia, you need to get over it. There is only one way to conquer the fear and that is to plunge in.

How important is your Christmas party?

The Christmas party, of course, is symbolic. How lavish is yours? Do you throw a big one, inviting influential government officials, developers, friends, neighbors, and anyone you can think of? How much did it cost you last year? We are not saying that you should not throw a Christmas party, but keep in mind that this is not marketing. If you wish to put the Christmas party on your expenses in your general ledger under promotion—because that is where you legally need to place it in order for it to be deductible—that is another matter.

Generally speaking those who are attending the party already know about you. Remember, the purpose of advertising is to let people know that you have the services they need. True, the party does enhance your image (we discuss image in another section) and it does remind people of your existence. But the question remains, How many jobs can you actually attribute to your last Christmas party that you would not have gotten by simply picking up the telephone, calling the individual, arranging an appointment, and meeting face to face?

Again, do not misunderstand. If you want to have a Christmas party, by all means do so. If you want to spend massive amounts of money, and your profits for the year are such that you can afford to do this, throw a great Christmas party and have fun! But do not delude yourself into thinking that you are effectively marketing your services. If the choice is to spend the money on a Christmas party or spend it on the tools necessary to do effective marketing, we both know that in reality there is no choice.

The $50,000 brochure is a symbol of success.

Image is very important for the architectural or engineering firm, as we will discuss in a later chapter. Firms often spend an outrageous amount of money for the design and production of their corporate brochure. The issue here is not the amount of money that is spent; it is whether or not available resources can be put to best use by doing this. A brochure is an important item for a professional firm. It should be well done, transmitting to potential clients the idea that this is a firm with which they would like to do business. At the same time, it is not a substitute for other marketing techniques. Many firms overdo their brochure because, like the Christmas party, it is easier and more non-threatening than other techniques. It also helps to feed the ego of the owner of the firm, who enjoys looking at his own brochure, his elegant office, and other trappings of success. Keep in mind, however, that this is not marketing.

Do you follow up or do you leave them alone?

Most architects or engineers, after an initial presentation, have absolutely no idea about what to do next. The general response from their potential clients is, "We liked it very much, it was very interesting, we are going to give it the utmost consideration, thank you very much." At that point the architect or engineer returns to his office and waits passively. If there is any follow-up at all, it generally goes something like this. A telephone call is made to the potential client: "Well, did you think it over?" or "I was just calling to see where you were on the project." The typical answer is, "We have not had time to consider it," or "We are having a meeting shortly," or some other put-off. Remember, the client usually has more put-offs than you have follow-ups. What most architectural or engineering firms need are proven methods to move the client off dead center, to test to see how much interest there really is on the part of the client, to ferret out objections to the proposal, to satisfy those objections, and to move to a successful conclusion. Follow-up is absolutely essential. Rarely does the client call you back himself.

Club membership helps you meet the right people.

Like the Christmas party and the $50,000 brochure, there is absolutely nothing wrong with having a club membership. Clubs may get you contacts, afford you a place to take a client to dinner, and provide a nice atmosphere conducive to business, but, as with most of the previously mentioned items, they are not a substitute for good sound marketing strategies. We are not saying that you should not have a club membership. It is just that if you are answering yes to many of these questions and they make up the vast majority of your marketing efforts, you are not really marketing effectively.

Membership in professional societies is absolutely essential.

These society affiliations, when properly noted on your brochures, handouts, business cards, proposals, and so forth, add a degree of credibility to your firm's image, and therefore you should belong to as many professional groups as you wish.

Are you the better mousetrap?

If you ask principals in architectural or engineering firms what their primary purpose within their organization is, they generally will tell you it is marketing. This is the way it should be. No one is going to market your professional services or the professional services of your firm better than you yourself. Over the years, we have worked with literally hundreds of architects and engineers in a variety of types of A/E firms and what we have found in a review of their time sheets is that the phase task code for marketing operations makes up sometimes as much as 30 to 60 percent of their time. This is wonderful if they have been actually marketing. Our findings, however, are that most principals in A/E firms use their marketing or promotion phase task code for any activity that under normal circumstances would be considered other indirect time. It is not that they are being dishonest on their time sheets. In fact many of them actually believe that any activity they engage in other than direct work on projects is for the purpose of marketing.

This belief, however, is based on a half truth. Clients dealing with a professional firm feel more comfortable (not to mention important) working directly with the owner; they know their account or their project will be handled by someone who is in authority, someone who in their opinion is the most professional person in that firm. This impression must indeed be constantly fostered. The client must never be made to feel that the owner is taking less than a personal interest in the project.

Remember, however, that marketing is selling the client on your professional services. Most people do not pick a firm based on the extraordinary reputation of the owner. Therefore they must be looking for something else. There are many factors that enter into their decision: price, performance, professionalism, production, efficiency, and so on. All these things go into making the final decision.

Most purchases, whether of architectural or engineering services or of an automobile, house, or even a box of cereal, are made on an emotional level. They are then rationalized after the decision to buy has been made. Some of the things that are going to help rationalize a client's decision to use your firm are your professional credentials, other projects you have done, the referrals you have, and you yourself—in their mind, the best architect or engineer they could get to perform the services. Do not delude yourself into thinking that these are the real reasons clients come to your firm to begin with. The reason they come is because of some previous marketing efforts. Unfortunately, most architects and engineers are unaware of even the good marketing efforts they make.

Do you have a patron?

This may sound like a strange question, but we have found that many temporarily successful A/E firms seem to have one (or maybe two) primary patrons that contribute 85 to 90 percent of the business of the firm. There is nothing wrong with this per se, but over a period of time the architects or engineers seem to feel uncomfortable with that relationship. As a result, they tend to cater less and less to the firm that has been responsible for their success. This is wrong. No firm ever went broke because it had too many clients willing to pay large fees. What can occur in a firm that has a patron is that the firm begins to focus solely on that patron, working so hard for that one company and placing all its efforts into keeping that one client happy, that it does not take the time to do any marketing whatsoever.

In architectural or engineering professional practices, marketing efforts do not pay off immediately. This is what makes it so difficult. Unlike large retailing firms, which can put a Sunday special ad in a local newspaper for Monday only or have a one-day clearance sale to draw in a flock of customers, A/E firms usually do not see the immediate results of their marketing efforts, which can take anywhere from three to six months before they become apparent. Therefore, marketing efforts can never cease.

Keep in mind that failure to market properly while doing work for the patron client who is keeping you in business is placing your company's future at risk. Eventually the client may become disenchanted with you, see a slump in his own business, or begin feeling that your firm is not large enough to handle his business, and, as a result, give you less work or drop you altogether. There is also a danger in terms of receivables. When you are dependent upon one client, any major holdup in receivables from this client can mean the end of your cash flow. Therefore, the more work one client gives you, the more marketing you must do in order to gain new clients to avoid any possible disruption by this one client, which may in turn create devastating effects on your firm.

Is community involvement good for business?

This is one place where most A/E firms shine in their marketing ability, but they also often make this their sole marketing effort. Community involvement is extremely important. It is through this involvement that you meet and make good contacts. This is especially true if you are pursuing government projects and contracts.

It does not matter whether you are a member of the Lions Club, the Rotary Club, or any other service organization, or whether your community involvement means donating your time or that of your firm for professional services at a reduced rate, at cost, or for free. This should be done and will reap rewards in the future.

As mentioned earlier, the purpose of this exercise is to help you paint a mental picture of what your firm is currently doing in the realm of marketing. If you see too many of your activities falling into the above categories, the bulk of your marketing is too one-sided. There is nothing wrong with them, but they must be put into perspective so that you can properly evaluate exactly where your advertising and marketing dollars are being spent. As will be discussed in the following sections, these activities should be used in balance with other marketing activities to get your name and message across to your potential clients. Rarely will one single activity in the above list, in and of itself, pick up a client.

The first thing that you should do for your firm is to go through these activities and cost out a dollar amount on each as though it were a project. This will enable you to see exactly how much it is costing you for your parties, brochures, club memberships, professional society dues, and community involvement. See what percentage these activities represent of your overall marketing budget. Evaluate your concept of advertising and salesmanship. How much follow-up do you do? How much breadth does your company have in the way of clients? Are you dependent on two or three clients for your existence? It is through evaluating what kind of firm you have, what kind of individual you are, where your firm is, and what you are doing to help promote your firm and get new clients that you will appreciate just exactly how much marketing you must do. It is not easy and it is not always fun, but it is undoubtedly the lifeblood of any A/E practice.

What Is Marketing?

Marketing can be thought of as a four-legged animal. The four aspects of marketing that we are going to discuss in this section are public relations, advertising, market analysis, and selling. As you are now aware, public relations is the easiest part of marketing and the one you currently feel the most comfortable with. It is where most of your marketing dollars and resources have been placed in the past. We will be the first to admit that public relations is an absolutely essential element of marketing, for a firm without good public relations and good image cannot successfully compete in today's marketplace. But it is not everything—public relations in and of itself never sold anything.

PUBLIC RELATIONS

The purpose of public relations is to produce an image. In the end, what you want is that anytime people hear your name or the name of your firm, they will immediately have a built-in concept of your firm as being the leader in your industry. The reason that this is necessary is because you are going to advertise. Advertising is more effective if the potential client has already heard of you and has a good impression of your firm. Therefore the purpose of public relations is to reinforce this image. When you advertise, when you send letters to potential clients, when you send them a brochure, and when you make a proposal, they will have a built-in appreciation of you and an emotional confirmation that they are doing the right thing. This is absolutely essential.

Therefore what you have been doing all along is right: you have been reinforcing your advertising. Keep in mind, however, that if you ignore other aspects of marketing, all your public relations activities will have been in vain.

ADVERTISING

Advertising is letting clients know that you exist. It is letting potential clients know what your services are and what you can possibly do for them. It is an attempt to make potential clients want to meet and talk with you. To show you the power of advertising for professional firms, let us give you an example.

We once worked with a school district that became disenchanted with a local architect for one reason or another. The primary discussion at school board meetings for the next several months was how to go about finding another architect for an upcoming school campus the board wanted to build. No one on the school board knew an architect. We had not even received correspondence from another architect for the last four or five years. In desperation, the school board went to the *Yellow Pages* to see who had the best ad. Needless to say, a few years ago there were no ads for architects, only name listings. Hundreds of them.

The next step was to call other school districts to find out which architect they were using and get their recommendations. Unfortunately, the recommendations of the other districts were for the same architect we were trying to get rid of. Finally, word got out that the school board was looking, and the first architect to knock on the door was invited in for an interview with the board of trustees and awarded the contract to build the new school.

What do you think would have happened if an architectural firm had sent even one letter to the school district or dropped by to meet the superintendent? Needless to say, that would have been the first architect to have been contacted. And under these circumstances, if that architect had given a good sales presentation, he would have been the one awarded the project. Even something as simple as this can produce spectacular results.

MARKET ANALYSIS

Before you are going to be able to effectively advertise, you will need to do a market analysis to determine exactly what it is you are selling. There are some standard steps you can take in order to do this.

1. *Identify your customers*. This step of your market survey requires a lot of work. Incredible as it sounds, you should make a list of the names and addresses of every possible client you could ever have. This is a mammoth task, but we never said it

was going to be easy. Next, take this list and begin building it into a computer data base.

2. *What is your product?* If you are an MEP engineer, your product is mechanical, electrical, and plumbing expertise. If you are an architect, your product is architectural services. In every industry, there are specializations. Is your work primarily residential, multifamily, commercial, subdivisions, strip centers, hospitals, or governmental agencies? What type of professional services do you offer? If you are an engineer, exactly what are the services that you provide? What is the scope of these services? What is it that you can do for your client?

These are not questions you will be able to answer in ten words or less. If you go into a new car showroom, there is not a salesman there who cannot list every possible option that he has to sell, how much it costs, and why it is good or not good for your particular purchase. This is what you need to put down in writing about your own firm. You need to outline exactly what it is that you do, and eventually you are going to need to find out what fee you need to charge to perform these services that you do so well. Until you have written down exactly what it is that you are selling, you have no way of directing the type of advertising you should undertake.

If one of your potential clients specializes in developing commercial strip centers, then you should aim your advertising literature, at least in part, toward such a developer. Advertising with specific markets in mind is more effective than simply a generic letter saying, "I am an architect and would appreciate your business."

As an architect or engineer, you have one big advantage over a general retailer in that your potential marketplace and client base is limited. On the surface, you may think of this as a disadvantage. Only 1 to 2 percent of an entire city's population will ever directly use architectural or engineering services (that is why you are probably not going to advertise on television). This is an advantage because the numbers are so small relative to the entire population that you are going to be able to direct your advertising specifically to the people who are going to use these professional services. And because the numbers are so small, you can also focus in on the needs of the particular client or group of clients you wish to reach. Therefore, you must list, in writing, exactly what it is you wish to sell to whom. Until you make that decision and know what it is that you want to market, you cannot expect to be successful.

3. *How much do you charge?* Are you charging too much? Are you charging too little? Do you perform your work on flat fee, percentage of construction cost, straight hourly, hourly to a maximum, or square foot basis? What do other firms in your area charge? What is your fee position in relationship to other A/E firms in your area? Which of the above-mentioned fee schedules is most profitable for your firm? What is the professional fee income of other firms in your area? What is your overhead rate? Is it higher or lower than that of other A/E firms? Have other A/E firms automated and to what extent? How do you compare? If you do not know the answers to each and every one of these questions, and have the answers down in writing in an organized manner, you are groping in the dark when you advertise, when you market, when you sell, when you negotiate your contracts, and when you perform your services. It is absolutely essential that you know your position in the marketplace relative to your competition. Without accurate information, there is no way you can effectively compete.

SELLING

Until you can get the client to say yes, until you can get the client to commit to the services of your firm, and until you can get the client to sign the contract that you have been negotiating, you have absolutely nothing.

Selling is the name of the game, no matter what the game. You can have a good image and wonderful public relations. You can have a great advertising campaign together with extensive information from your market survey. But until you can sell the client and convince him that what you have to offer is in his best interest, and until you get the client emotionally involved in the decision, you have absolutely nothing.

It never ceases to amaze us just how little architects and engineers know about the business of selling. Although we will provide a section later in this part to acquaint you with some of the basic aspects of sales, we strongly encourage any professional to read other books, attend seminars, take courses, and practice good professional selling techniques.

One of the hardest things for people to do in life is to make a decision, even one that is good for them. Most people need help and that is what selling is. Unless you understand the psychology of helping people to make a decision and of getting them involved in the decision, you are not doing your clients a service.

MARKETING BUDGET

How much are you spending on marketing? If you have not done so, take time at this point to go back and look at your general ledger for the past year to see exactly how much has been classified under the category of marketing, promotion, advertising, public relations, and so on. Once you have the figure for the past year, go back and look at the individual transactions. Subtract office parties, luncheons, entertainment, and other things that in all honesty are really not part of promoting your company. Now take a look at this figure.

You will need one more figure from your general ledger to see exactly what your ratio for marketing is. That is your total gross revenue less cost of direct expenses or reimbursable items (other than direct labor). What we want to arrive at is a gross revenue figure that is not contaminated by things (direct consultant costs and other things that are pass-through items, generally reimbursable by your client) that in a retail environment would be considered cost of goods sold. A good formula would be (Gross Professional Revenue) + (Reimbursable Revenue) − (All Direct Expenses Other Than Direct Labor). This equals your total project-related revenue. Divide this total revenue into your total marketing figure. This gives you the percentage of marketing to revenue. Is it 10 percent? Is it 5 percent? Less than 1 percent? Generally speaking, if your marketing efforts are 5 to 10 percent of your total income from professional services, you are spending the right amount.

Of your marketing efforts, what percentage is public relations, as we have previously defined it, and what percentage is direct advertising efforts? Remember that public relations is your brochures, community involvement, professional societies, club memberships, and the like. Direct advertising is made up of presentations before a client, mailers or letters to potential clients, advertising directed at specialized client markets, and so on. If your public relations expense is more than 30 percent of your entire marketing budget, it is too large.

Needless to say, there are no absolute percentages that you should adhere to, but there are some basic rules of thumb. Public relations should make up no more than 20 to 30 percent of your marketing budget. Direct advertising should be a full 50 percent or more. Approximately 10 to 20 percent of your marketing dollars should be spent toward direct contact and selling to the client.

Chances are, if yours is a typical A/E firm, 80 percent or more of your entire marketing budget is dedicated to public relations activities. It is simply common sense to reduce this figure, create priorities, and do those things that will have direct results in getting you to meet the client and giving you the opportunity to sell to the client. Until you can make a proposal to a client, you have no chance of getting a project.

Marketing A/E services is not really different from any other marketing activity. There are numbers and ratios involved. The more presentations you make, the better your chances of being awarded a contract. Therefore, the more effort you put into attracting the people to make presentations to, the better your chances of getting to make these presentations. Letting potential clients know exactly what it is that you can do for them and why they need to talk to you is where your primary effort should be focused. Keep priorities in mind. Public relations is meant to back up direct advertising and selling. You should not ignore your image, but if it is to do any good, your primary efforts must be in direct advertising.

OVERALL OBJECTIVE

Do you have goals? Do you know what it is that you want to do? If you do not, how do you know when you have accomplished it? Do you know what it is you are working toward? Write your goals down. You must write down how many proposals you wish to make, how many people you need to talk to, and how many people you need to contact. This *must* be in writing. How many projects do you want? Once you know what it is you want to do, how many people you must contact in order to do this, and how many proposals you must make, it is much easier to proceed and reach your goals.

If over the next 6 months your firm must secure 10 new projects with an average fee of $20,000 to $50,000 each, how many proposals do you need to put out? The answer may be 100, 80, or 50. It does not matter. You should be able to look back over your past records and see how many projects you have received based upon how many proposals you have issued. If you need to issue 50 proposals to reach your goal, then how many people do you have to talk to in order to issue a proposal? Maybe 100, maybe 200. Whatever it is, you need to know that number. Once you know that over the next 6 months you must talk to 100 individuals, your next goal is to contact more than 100 individuals, send them letters and information, try to get them to call you, call them to see if they got the information, and try to arrange a time for you to drop by to see them.

All businesses revolve around numbers. If yours is a civil engineering firm with shorter contract periods and you perform projects in one week to one month, needless to say your fee for each project will not be as high as that of an architectural firm with six-month to one-year projects. The numbers for each industry, and even each firm, will vary. You must know your numbers and write them down in relationship to your objectives and goals.

By writing down goals and objectives, you are creating a road map to keep you on track and to secure positive reinforcement as each milestone is reached. And an interesting thing happens once you write goals down and begin working toward them: you will far surpass what you have been doing in the past.

Who Is the Client?

In establishing your target market it is absolutely essential that you know who your client is. We stated in the last chapter that we wanted you to make a list of every potential client that you could possibly have in your area. This might sound ridiculous, but it is vital. Until you know who your potential clients are, there is no way for you to directly advertise to them. If you do not know who they are, how do you expect them to know who you are and what you have to offer them? The potential clients of architects and engineers can be divided into three areas: the private sector, the public sector, and others.

PRIVATE SECTOR

Real estate developers: Obviously real estate developers and builders need and use architects and engineers. Real estate developers are a prime source of clients if for no other reason than there are so many of them.

Commercial developers: Like real estate developers, commercial developers have been the mainstay of many A/E firms for a continuous stream of business, especially in cities where commercial business has been booming. Unfortunately, the problem is that they tend to go through boom-or-bust periods. When times get tight or difficult and commercial developers' names appear in newspapers for bankruptcy cases, many architects and engineers fail to recognize that times will not always be tough for this particular segment of the economy. It is also true that, even in the bleakest of times when well-known names are having difficulties, new and unheard of developers are coming in to pick up the scraps.

The challenge in marketing directly to real estate and commercial developers is to find the new ones. Many times this is extremely difficult. Most developers keep a very low profile. They are very secretive and prefer their dealings to be strictly confidential. As a result, you cannot simply turn to the *Yellow Pages* under commercial and real estate developers to find them. As we will discuss a little later, there are techniques for ferreting out these individuals. The point we wish to make at this time is that they should not be ignored, because they are now, and may always be, the mainstay of many A/E firms.

Private companies or franchises: There seems to be a general rotation in the business market. Even when real estate and commercial developers have fallen on hard times, it does not mean that nothing is being built in your city or geographical area. A/E firms must constantly be on the lookout for other potential clients. One excellent area for this is private companies or franchises, especially those individuals who are going to be opening up a new business and/or building their own building, whether it be, for example, a restaurant, a nursing home, a small medical complex, or a theater. These are individuals with private businesses who need architectural design, space planning, and engineering for their own property, which they are building for their own private and commercial use.

Major chains: Although many major chains have their own architectural or engineering staff to produce the initial design for their stores, they also hire local architects and engineers because it is more economical to do so. Marketing to major chains needs to be done at the corporate office level.

Major chains include restaurants, hotels, motels, banks, other financial institutions, department stores, and so on. We know of one architect who has made his living and has built a good, profitable business by doing nothing but pizza parlors. Although this is not glamorous and may not win any design awards, his firm has had a steady stream of work from one major chain.

Private institutions: Private institutions are primarily nonprofit businesses that are still in the private rather than the public sector, for example, churches, which are constantly engaged in building programs. Basically, private nonpublic institutions build for their own purposes in a not-for-profit environment. Other private institutions might be private schools or hospitals, to name but two examples.

PUBLIC SECTOR

Federal government: Needless to say the federal government hires more architects and engineers than anyone else. Of course the government hires more of *everything* than everyone else. Although it has its own architects and engineers, there is still a mass of work available to those who know how to market to the government and go out and get it. To make matters even easier for you, the federal government publishes, on a weekly basis, a list of projects that are coming up for every branch of the government.

City/state governments: When pursuing city business, you should personally meet every single individual in the city government hierarchy who has any authority regarding which architect or engineer is selected for any project. This includes not only those departments involved with potential projects, but also the city council or governing board in your area. In any given area, there are not that many people involved. At the state level, unless you happen to reside in the capital city, state government officials may be placed in the same procedural category as the federal government.

School districts: Every school district in the United States needs to build something. It may be a new high school or a new gymnasium or an athletic facility or a garage for the buses, but every school district sooner or later will build something. In some states there may be only 1 or 2 school districts, while others may have 50 or 60, and yet others as many as 200. The point is this: There is no excuse for not making direct contact with every superintendent of every school district within your state.

Public institutions: Public institutions include any institution that is either wholly or partially tax supported. These include universities, hospitals, jails, prisons, and so forth. Needless to say, these public institutions may cross other areas, such as city/state, and come under general governmental rules concerning proposals for municipal and state projects. Others, such as special taxing districts, water districts, and utility boards, may have their own jurisdictional requirements and might possibly be able to give out contracts independently of other city or state agencies.

OTHERS

Architects: If you are an engineer, chances are that one of your potential clients is an architect. In fact, for many projects engineers are consultants to architects: the architect becomes the primary client and the engineer never interfaces with the end user. Even if you are an architect, you might find that other architects need your services. You should never ignore marketing directly to other architects, even though they may be your competition. Joint venture projects are extremely common. Obviously, the type of direct advertising that you do aimed at a potential competitor is quite different from the direct advertising that is directed at other target markets.

Other professionals—limited partnerships: Successful professionals—doctors, lawyers, even architects and engineers—are constantly looking for ways to protect their money because most tax shelters have been closed by the Internal Revenue Service. The last successful haven to shelter income is real estate. One such vehicle for investors has been the limited partnership. This limited partnership may be put together by one of the professionals, by a real estate developer, a commercial developer, or possibly an architectural or engineering firm. The purpose of the limited partnership is to pool money on a partnership basis for a potential investment in a manner that will limit the risk of the individual partners to the sum total of their investment. There is always a general partner who accepts the risk and manages the limited partnership, in return receiving a commission for his managerial expertise.

A limited partnership can invest in anything. Many of these limited partnerships build things. Except in a very economically active area, it is very rare for limited partnerships to buy raw land and retain it undeveloped for years with the hopes of turning the property undeveloped (however, this can happen in an area of economic boom). Most limited partnerships tend to turn their investments in no more than five years and many of them are interested during the holding period in gaining income from the investment to offset expenses before they sell it. Of course, any development usually requires the services of an architect or an engineer.

FINDING YOUR CLIENTS

Once you have decided what sector your future clients belong in, whether it is public, private, other, or a combination of all three, you must begin getting the names and addresses and telephone numbers of all of your potential clients.

A computer can help you organize lists of names and addresses, sort through them, write individual letters, mailmerge those names with letters, and track vital tickler dates. It is as essential an element of a productive office as your typewriter. You should use at the very least microcomputer data base operations to manage this list. (We will be talking in terms of a data base as it relates to microcomputers. There are many data base programs on the market and any one of them will suffice for these purposes. If you are not familiar with data bases or how they work, go to any computer store for additional information.)

We are going to be building two major data bases. The first one will be general clients and client contacts, and the second will be other architectural and engineering firms.

We have said many times that you must meet your clients before you can have any hope of securing business from them, but one of the things that we have not emphasized is that your potential clients usually have no desire, at this point, to meet you. Therein lies the challenge. The data base that we intend to build will not be built overnight. It is going to be a continuous and tedious process, done daily and/or weekly.

Any time you find a new client and/or potential client, your data base must be updated. Basically there will be two types of clients in your client data base.

The first group is what we will call general contacts; the second consists of your actual potential or existing clients. You should not really expect the general contacts themselves to turn into clients (of course, this is not to say that they will not). They are people who know people who know people who need architectural or engineering services. A general contact can be literally anyone. You never know who you will meet who knows somebody who happens to be engaged in a building project. Therefore, your purpose in marketing is to present your story directly to as many people as you can, even if those people have no need whatsoever for architectural or engineering services.

On the other side of the data base are those people who are going to be your actual clients.

How do you find these people? The first thing you should do is to get out your telephone directory, turn to the various industries you are interested in contacting, and enter their names and addresses from the telephone book into your data base.

Another good source is the newspaper, not only the major ones, but also community newspapers. Many newspapers have columns, usually in the business section, such as "On The Move," "New Openings," "Business Announcements," and the like. Whatever your particular newspaper calls these columns, they generally operate as a forum for people to publicize their own achievements: new products they are releasing, promotions within their organization, new locations and leases that have been signed, new business ventures. All of these types of announcements and articles usually include the name of both the individual and the business. Other beneficial sources are the women's lifestyle and community neighborhood news sections (each newspaper has its own name for these), business articles, and, of course, real estate sections. The point of all this is that every person who gets mentioned in the newspaper for some achievement gives you an invitation to contact him or her. These are what we call general contacts. To each of these you will write a general introductory letter, like that in the following example:

Dear Mr. Jones:

Congratulations on (*whatever the achievement or focus of the newspaper article*). I know you are very proud of this particular achievement and I would like to take this opportunity to introduce myself.

(Brief description of yourself and your services.)

If I may be of any service to you or your firm, please don't hesitate to contact me. I would love the opportunity to meet you at some future time.

Sincerely,

Enter this information in your data base. You can build a data base and increase it by adding 5 to 15 names each day just with these general contacts. True, this is a tedious, time-consuming task, and not at all fun. It is also costly. Stamps and letterhead are not cheap. The fact is that if you got one major project that brought in a good fee out of all of these letters, it would be hard to imagine what the hourly rate of production of these letters would be. Remember, it is a numbers game. Clients do not take out ads that say, "I need an architect" or "I need an engineer." It is amazing how many people need architects or engineers, how many are interested in building something. This is one prime way to circulate in the business community.

One large group to put into your data base is every bank and savings and loan association in your entire state. There is a *Bankers Red Book* (produced by Bankers Digest, Inc.), which includes the name and title of each officer. These are general contacts that normally do not themselves use architects and engineers (unless the bank is currently involved in a building program). But the purpose here is not to directly sell A/E services to the bank officers. Rather, most developers, once a project is consolidated in their mind, consult a banker. And since bankers naturally have a vested interest in keeping abreast of the building industry, you should be their prime source of information.

Do a survey of the local apartment complexes in your area. (Look out, there may be hundreds of them!) Most apartment complexes are built by small companies, limited partnerships, and other small groups, as well as by commercial developers. Once you find out who the owners of the apartment complexes are, you have found a group interested in development. This same group may be involved in other projects.

Find out who is building. Go to the courthouse to see who has taken out building permits and copy this information weekly. If your city or county clerk's office provides you with this information in printed form, great; if not, do the legwork yourself. This is the one place that developers are required to register. They have no choice—they must become visible and report to this source. (This is not the time to go after a particular project—it is too late for that. What you are after here are the names for your data base.)

Make a list of every national franchise or chain that you can think of. Once you have done that, make a concentrated effort to find out where their home offices are and include them in your data base.

The names of major real estate brokers can usually be found in the real estate section of your local newspaper as well as in the telephone directory. But be selective: even in small cities, there may be a thousand or more real estate agents or brokers. Concentrate on the major ones, especially those who are involved in the sale or development of commercial property, and then cut this number down to a hundred. The top brokers in any major city generally are also involved, either directly or indirectly, with development.

Architects and engineers routinely receive requests for proposals (RFPs). Whether or not the RFP you receive from any individual or group interests you is immaterial (for this purpose); always add the source of any RFP to your data base.

Share your data base. There are many companies that are not involved in architectural or engineering professional sservices, but are people you do business with every day, people who are marketing to the same clients that you are marketing to, with different products. These might be people who handle your printing, office supplies, or retail purchases. And do not forget your banker. As long as you are not in competition with these individuals, why not exchange leads? Cooperation with noncompetitive groups can generate good leads. It can also be easier making initial contacts with the help of these individuals. They can give you names to be used as referrals.

As you can see, identifying and locating potential clients is not always easy. It is tedious, time-consuming, and sometimes costly work, but it is absolutely necessary if you are going to build a strong, healthy client base. The potential rewards can be tremendous.

Building the Data Base

As we have discussed before, a microcomputer is absolutely essential for any professional architectural or engineering firm. Since the cost of microcomputers has gone down, even the smallest firm can afford one. The amount of information that you are going to be gathering must be handled by some form of computer system. As you well know, computers may be used for a variety of purposes in automating an A/E office. We are going to concentrate on two specific uses centered around marketing: word processing and data base management.

Many A/E firms have used word processing for years. The ability of a good word processing program to handle correspondence and project specifications is well established. It really does not matter which word processing program you have as long as you feel comfortable with it. Our only requirement is that a word processing program have a mailmerge feature built directly into it. Mailmerge, as it is generically known, is an adjunct program that makes it possible to write a single form letter using variable names within the body of the letter and to merge other names from a data base to permit the computer to write a personalized letter to each name on the data base, using specific names in the body of the letter. Although this is not absolutely required, it does give a more personal touch to your mailings.

A data base management program is a specialized program capable of storing large amounts of information about given individuals. Data base programs range in price from $200 to $800, depending on the complexity and sophistication of the program. For our purposes, the data base program need not be overly complicated or sophisticated. We have tried many data base programs over the years and have found that most A/E firms are usually better off with a less sophisticated but easier to use program. You do not want to spend all your time becoming a computer programmer in order to secure information from your data base. If you are not familiar with these programs, any local computer store will be happy to assist you.

One standard feature of all data base programs is that the program creates a file containing information on like subjects. We are going to be maintaining two major data base files. The first file is going to be for potential clients, existing clients, or general contacts. The second is going to be a file on your competitors, other A/E firms.

A data base is divided into what is known as fields. Basically fields are small pieces of information, such as company name, address, city, state, zip code, type of client, and so on. (Note that individual firm in the data base will have the same fields as all other firms in the data base, whether or not these fields are necessary.) In most data bases a field must have a field name and a designated size. The size of a field is measured by the number of bytes it contains. One byte is equal to one letter/space/number. Simply stated, if you want a field named "company name" and you designate that field to be 30 bytes long, what you have said is that you need room to type in 30 characters for the company name. We are not going to elaborate here on how to use the various data base programs because there are too many of them available. You will need to consult the manual on your data base program for specific instructions.

The following are recommended sample fields for the two data bases that we are going to cover. The sample data bases we have created here are by no means the final word on what should or should not be in your own data base. They are only recommendations, samples to be used as a guideline. The particular data base that you set up may have more or fewer fields and should be customized to your own needs. We do recommend, however, that whatever data base program you purchase, be sure you have the capability of adding fields and expanding the data base as your needs require. Also, avoid data bases that destroy existing data if you have to change the number or size of fields involved.

DATA BASE FOR POTENTIAL CLIENTS

Company name; field size, 30. This is simply the name of the company. Remember to type in the information as you would like it to appear on the inside address of a letter or on a mailing label.

Street address; field size, 30. Notice here that we have provided only one field for the street address rather than two. With most data base programs it is very difficult to have a second street address field if it is not always used. Without proper program-

Figure 3

Data Base of Potential Clients: Entry Form

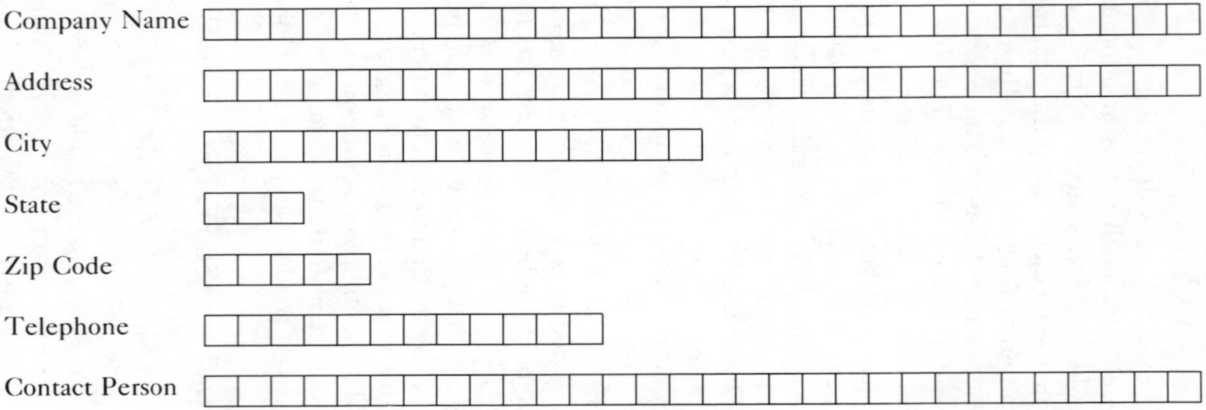

Company Name

Address

City

State

Zip Code

Telephone

Contact Person

Type of Record ☐

1. General Contact
2. Potential Client
3. Client

Type of Client ☐

1. Real Estate Developer
2. Commercial Developer
3. School District
4. Church
5. Franchise
6. Small Business

Type of Contact ☐

1. Low Level
2. Decision Maker

Referred By

Source ☐

1. Newspaper
2. Yellow Pages
3. Business Directory
4. Telephone Survey
5. RFP
6. Referral

Date Entered

Memo:

Figure 4

Data Base of A/E Firms: Entry Form

Company Name

Address

City

State

Zip Code

Telephone

Contact Person

Type of Firm ☐

1. Architect
2. Engineer—Civil
3. Engineer—MEP
4. Surveyor
5. Engineer—Structural

Date Entered

Billing Rates:

Principal

Proj. Manager

Arch/Eng.

Draftsman

Clerical

Overhead Rate

Number Emp.

Automation:

CAD

Word Processing ☐ Accounting ☐ Proj. Management ☐

Memo:

DATA BASE: POTENTIAL CLIENTS

FIELD	SIZE
Company Name	30
Street Address	30
City	15
State	2
Zip Code	5
Telephone	12
Contact Person	30
Type of Record	1
1. General Contact	
2. Potential Client	
3. Client	
Type of Client	1
1. Real Estate Developer	
2. Commercial Developer	
3. School District	
4. Church	
5. Franchise	
6. Small Business	
Type of Contact	1
1. Low Level	
2. Decision Maker	
Referred by	30
Source	1
1. Newspaper	
2. Yellow Pages	
3. Business Directory	
4. Telephone Survey	
5. RFP	
6. Referral	
Date Entered	8

DATE OF CONTACT		TYPE CONTACT	
CD1	8	TYPE_C1	1
CD2	8	TYPE_C2	1
CD3	8	TYPE_C3	1
CD4	8	TYPE_C4	1
CD5	8	TYPE_C5	1
CD6	8	TYPE_C6	1
CD7	8	TYPE_C7	1
CD8	8	TYPE_C8	1

DATE OF CONTACT		TYPE CONTACT	
CD9	8	TYPE__C9	1
CD10	8	TYPE__C10	1

1. Telephone, you called
2. Telephone, they called you
3. Office visit, their office
4. Office visit, your office
5. Presentation
6. Proposal
7. Follow-up letter
8. Follow-up telephone

Date Last Direct Mailer	8
Mailer Code	10

PROJECTS		TYPE PROJECT		A/E FIRM	
PJ1	20	TYPJ1	3	AE1	30
PJ2	20	TYPJ2	3	AE2	30
PJ3	20	TYPJ3	3	AE3	30
PJ4	20	TYPJ4	3	AE4	30
PJ5	20	TYPJ5	3	AE5	30
PJ6	20	TYPJ6	3	AE6	30
PJ7	20	TYPJ7	3	AE7	30
PJ8	20	TYPJ8	3	AE8	30
PJ9	20	TYPJ9	3	AE9	30
PJ10	20	TYPJ10	3	AE10	30

Tickler Date 8

Memo ____

____

____

____

____

DATA BASE: A/E FIRMS

FIELD	SIZE
Company Name	30
Street Address	30
City	15
State	2

(continued)

DATA BASE: A/E FIRMS (continued)

FIELD	SIZE
Zip Code	5
Telephone	12
Contact Person	30
Type of Firm	1
1. Architect	
2. Engineer, Civil	
3. Engineer, MEP	
4. Surveyor	
5. Etc.	
Date Entered	8

PROJECTS		TYPE PROJECT		CLIENT		
PJ1	20	TYPJ1	3	CL1	30	
PJ2	20	TYPJ2	3	CL2	30	
PJ3	20	TYPJ3	3	CL3	30	
PJ4	20	TYPJ4	3	CL4	30	
PJ5	20	TYPJ5	3	CL5	30	
PJ6	20	TYPJ6	3	CL6	30	
PJ7	20	TYPJ7	3	CL7	30	
PJ8	20	TYPJ8	3	CL8	30	
PJ9	20	TYPJ9	3	CL9	30	
PJ10	20	TYPJ10	3	CL10	30	
Billing Rates						
1. Principal						8
2. Project manager						8
3. Architect/Engineer						8
4. Draftsman						8
5. Clerical						8
Overhead Rate						8
Number of Employees						3
Automation						
CAD						10
Word Processing						1
Accounting						1
Project Management						1
Tickler Date						8

Memo ____

____

____

____

____

ming, this can result in a blank skipped line. It is much more convenient to put all the address information on one line. Notice that the size (30 bytes) of both the company name and the street address may seem a bit limited. Depending upon the size of your mailing labels, you may be able to expand this to 35 bytes. Generally speaking, however, labels do not go beyond 40 characters, so be careful.

City: field size, 15. Enter the name of the city.

State: field size, 2. Only two bytes were given here, so you must use the two-character state abbreviation.

Zip code: field size, 5. Naturally if you wish to use the 9-digit zip code, make the field 10 bytes long (include an extra byte for the hyphen).

Telephone: field size, 12. The 12 bytes given here are used as follows: 3-digit area code, hyphen, 3-digit prefix, hyphen, 4-digit telephone number. If you wish to use parentheses around the area code, increase this field size to 13 bytes.

Contact person: field size, 30. The contact person is the individual that you have made, or should make, contact with within the firm. This could be considered as one field, with the entire name of the person at 30 bytes. Alternately, you may wish to break up the field to title, first name, and last name, and use it as three separate fields. By breaking up this field, you will have the advantage of being able to identify the last name and the first name separately in a mailmerge document.

Type of record: field size, 1. If you want to save space, you can use general codes in fields. For example, you might want to know what type of record this is. Is it for a potential client, an existing client, or a general contact? By creating a legend (1 = general contact, 2 = potential client, 3 = existing client), you can save space by simply entering a 1, 2, or 3. This also makes it very easy to change a general contact to a potential client or a potential client to a client by simply changing the coding number on the record.

Type of client: field size, 1. This field is used to identify the type of client you are marketing to. It is useful to have information in your data base as to whether the client is a real estate developer, commercial developer, school district, church, franchise, small business, or any other type of client you deal with.

Type of contact: field size, 1. This field is used primarily for potential clients. You will need to know whether the contact person has the ability to make decisions or whether your contact must receive permission from the decision maker in order to accept your proposal. Naturally it is in your best interest to graduate through the potential client's firm to a contact who is the decision maker.

Referred by: field size, 30. If this potential client was added to your data base because of a referral, you would write in the name of the individual or company making the referral.

Source: field size, 1. This field indicates how you came about this particular name in order to add it to the data base. As you can see from the legend, it can be by newspaper, *Yellow Pages,* business directory, and so on. You indicate the code in this field.

Date entered: field size, 8. All dates should contain 8 bytes. They represent a 2-digit month, slash, a 2-digit day, slash, and a 2-digit year.

Date of contact/type of contact: field size, 8/1. As you can see from our sample, we have recommended that you have as many as 10 different fields for date of contact. These should be paired with an accompanying 10 fields called type of contact. The date of contact requires 8 bytes and type of contact 1 byte. In many data base programs, you must have a completely separate field name for each field label. This can be accomplished by calling the date of contact CD1, CD2, CD3, and so on through CD10. Type of contact might be TYPE_C1 through TYPE_C10. (Notice the underlining here. Many data bases will not permit you to put spaces between words in a field label or field name. One way around this is to use an underline character as a space so that the data base program will recognize this as a legitimate character.) These two fields are usually used anytime you make an individual contact, or a personal contact with that potential client or general contact, and should not be used for mass mailers.

Some coding types might be telephone calls (you call them, or they call you), office visit (to their office, to your office), presentations, proposals, follow-up letters, follow-up telephone calls, initial congratulatory letters, and so forth. The purpose of these fields is not necessarily for search capabilities, but so that when you call the record up on the computer screen or get a hard copy printout, which we will create later, you will be able to see which contacts have been made in the past.

Date last direct mailer/mailer code: field size, 8/10. Part of your marketing campaign will be sending out mass mailings to various clients in various industries. As you send these out, you will need to input the date of the mailing, which will be 8 bytes, and a mailing code, which may be up to 10 bytes, as a description of the particular mailing piece that was sent out.

Projects/type project/A/E firm: field size, 20/3/30. As you gather information about your potential clients, you should input each project they have done, the type of project it is, and the A/E firm they used. Here again, each data base may differ but generally requires a separate field label for each category. Projects might be labeled PJ1 through PJ10, type of project might be labeled TYPJ1 through TYPJ10, and the A/E firm used might be AE1 through AE10. Needless to say, they should be lined up so that you can easily see that PJ1, TYPJ1, and AE1 all belong together.

Tickler date: field size, 8. This is a date that reminds you to do something. It could be when you should make contact again with the client, or send the client an additional mailer, or send more information, or it can be a proposal deadline date.

Memo. Your data base should permit you to make some type of memo entry on each record. This is basically a free field that may be virtually unlimited and that would provide enough space for you to write freestyle notes concerning a client. These notes might include a detailed record of conversations, things agreed upon, objections raised, or any other pertinent fact about the client that might be helpful before you make a telephone call or a personal visit.

DATA BASE FOR A/E FIRMS

As indicated previously, the data base for A/E firms is one that you will be keeping on your competition. The first items, company name and contact person, are directory information pieces and are essentially the same as the information that was provided in the potential client data base.

Type of firm: field size, 1 (or 2). This is where you enter the type of firm this is, whether architectural, engineering (may be divided into civil, MEP, structural), surveying, or whatever designation is meaningful to you.

Date entered: field size, 8. This is the same as the one in the client data base.

Projects/type project/client: field size, 20/3/30. This is essentially the same information as in the client data base under project/type project, except that it is for your competitors. It is here that you will list their major projects and what type of projects these are. Also list the client of the A/E firm for the indicated project. One of the uses that we are going to make of this information is in cross-referencing clients with A/E firms and A/E firms with clients to see which potential clients are using more than one A/E firm. As you will see, clients who use more than one architect or engineer for various projects are open to working with multiple A/E firms—or might be easily disenchanted with the firms they work with.

Billing rates: field size, 8. You will need an individual field for each of the types of classifications and billing rates. These classifications might include principal, project manager, architect or engineer (depending upon what kind of firm it is), draftsman, technician (depending upon the classification buzzwords in your area), clerical, and the like.

Overhead rate: field size, 8. One of the most valuable pieces of information you can have on your competition is their firm's overhead rate. If you know the overhead rate of a company, you can easily determine such information as the minimum amount they are able to bid on any given project.

Number of employees: field size, 3. This is the total number of employees employed by the A/E firm.

Automation. You may need multiple fields for this, depending upon the type of information you would like to have. For example, it might be very useful to know if they have a CAD system. Naturally this would affect the amount they would be able to bid on a project and the resulting profit they would make. Other pieces of information concerning automation might be word processing, accounting, and project management.

Tickler date: field size, 8. This is the same as for the client data base.

Memo. This is also the same as for the client data base.

It is absolutely essential that you begin creating your data bases as soon as possible because they are going to be the crux of your entire marketing campaign. These data bases will provide you with an organized way to list potential clients and to systematically make contact with them. Rome was not built in a day—

and neither will these data bases be. You may wish to start with the names you find in your telephone directory and go on from there. Keep the information up to date. Review the newspaper daily and make a list of the individuals who have been written up. Make your data base as useful a tool as possible.

Intelligence

It is our firm belief that the more information you have on the operation of your competitors and your potential clients, the better you will be able to compete. In this chapter we are going to outline some techniques for acquiring this information, and it is up to you which ones you use. Our one suggestion is that you be honest and aboveboard at all times.

This chapter deals with a very sensitive area. All of the information contained here may not be suitable for everyone. It is not our intent to offend anyone or to suggest that you do anything that, in your opinion, may be questionable. Nor is it our intent to judge what is ethical for you to do in business. Naturally we do not recommend anything that is illegal. You may wish, after reading the material in this chapter, to adopt some, none, part, or all of the information contained herein. This will, of course, be your decision.

TECHNIQUE #1: TELEPHONE SURVEY

This first technique is a very straightforward one. You are simply going to ask questions. Needless to say, if you call a local competitor and ask them what their overhead rate is, you may get a cold silence on the other end of the phone as the receptionist puts you through to the principal, who is going to want to know who you are and why you want that information. There are only a limited number of questions you are going to be able to ask over the telephone without arousing undue concern.

Let us begin with the telephone survey. This should be done in a very straightforward, businesslike manner, but with a warm friendly voice. There are not many questions you can expect people to answer over the telephone. What you can get is their mailing address, the name of a principal (contact person), and number of employees. But it does not have to end there. If they ask you who you are and why you want this information, feel perfectly free to tell them the name of your firm and that you are doing a telephone survey of other architectural or engineering firms in the area for a possible future joint venture. This is not a misstatement of fact because you can honestly say that if the situation and financial arrangements were right, you would be more than happy to enter into a joint venture with another A/E firm. Depending upon the reception you get, you might then feel free to ask questions concerning their automation, and maybe even chat with them about how they like the system they have.

The telephone survey can be a very powerful tool if used correctly. Chances are that the receptionist who answers the telephone is not going to know a great deal about the firm's project-related automation. This will have to come from an individual higher up. Therefore it is very easy and natural for you as the owner of a firm (now that you have the name of a contact person) to simply call that individual and ask for some help. This is especially easy if you have found that they have a CAD system. Call the principal (or contact person) of the firm, tell him that you understand that he has a CAD system, and discuss with him how he went about making that decision. You can get some extremely useful information with this line of conversation. Naturally, financial considerations and the amount of money a CAD system can save a firm had to have been one of those important factors in his decision to make that purchase.

Emphasize that you have talked with several people who wish to sell you a CAD system and that you cannot get a good answer to the question of exactly how that cost is going to be recouped, especially if you do primarily hourly projects. You will be amazed how much information the owner of another firm, when approached in this manner, will give you in order to brag about the in-depth study his firm did, and how they are recouping the cost of the CAD system. What it boils down to is this: There are only two ways to recoup the cost of a CAD system for an architectural or engineering firm.

1. If you work with flat fee projects, the cost is recouped by bidding out the project as if it were being done in the traditional, manual manner. By using the CAD system, you can spend fewer actual hours and come in under budget.
2. If you emphasize hourly projects, the only other way to recoup the cost of a CAD system used on an hourly project is to bill out the CAD system separately.

If you ask this firm how they do that and they say they bill out their CAD system separately, you now know they emphasize hourly projects. Ask the principal what he feels would be a fair billing rate for the CAD system. Chances are he will tell you whether they are actually billing it out or not. In a very naive voice, simply ask if the CAD system rate should be equal to half of or a certain percentage of what you would normally bill for a draftsman, for example. As long as this is done in a natural manner and you are appreciative of the information this principal is giving you (and you will be!), he will most likely continue to answer most of your questions gladly. If you handle this correctly, you will get the billing rates for this firm for a wide variety of employee classifications. One word of caution: Do not push. If you detect any reluctance on the part of an architect or engineer to supply you with the information you request, channel your conversation back to the general merits of the CAD system. As an aside, you will be surprised how much you can learn about the true value and merits of a CAD system if you do not already own one.

Remember, you are not being dishonest. We feel confident that you can honestly say that you would be very interested in knowing what they think of their system, and how they are using it to help their office automation and to increase the profitability of their company. Any information that they give will be offered freely to someone truthfully identifying himself.

TECHNIQUE #2: ANSWERING CLASSIFIED ADS

If you do not already own a crisscross directory of your city, please get one. They are relatively inexpensive (about $100 per year) and are updated annually. It will surprise you how much information you can secure from a directory such as this and how comforting it is, when returning a call where all you have is the telephone number, to know in advance who it is that you are calling. We, however, are going to use the crisscross directory for another purpose: answering classified ads. You should always read the classified ads under any category an A/E firm would use when hiring. Needless to say there are various A/E firms in your area that are advertising for architects, engineers, draftsmen, clerical staff, and so on. They may or may not indicate exactly which company it is. This is where the crisscross directory comes in. Look up the telephone number so that you will have the information available for your data base without having to identify the firm by telephoning. Call on the ad. You are in control. Ask for as much information about the position as would be valuable to you. This is fair game. They have publicly advertised and solicited calls. Anyone calling on the ad has the perfect right to ask how much it pays, what the duties are, what types of projects the new employee would be working on, and so forth. They will either answer your questions or not. A word of caution: Do not have one of your own employees answer the ads . . . they may take the job!

TECHNIQUE #3: DIRECT MAIL QUESTIONNAIRE

This is a very straightforward technique. It is simply a direct mail questionnaire to all architectural and engineering firms in your area, prefaced by a letter indicating that the reason you are sending the questionnaire is that you have some possible presentations coming up and are interested in joint ventures for some of them. Add that in order to become better acquainted with their firm, you would appreciate it if they would take the time to answer the questions and return the form to you. In this questionnaire, anything is fair game. Include questions on past projects, preferred method of billing, special requirements for joint ventures, automation, and the like. Some firms will answer, some will not. Some firms will answer only some of the questions. The results you receive from this questionnaire will indeed surprise you and give you valuable information.

TECHNIQUE #4: PUBLIC RECORDS

As you are probably aware, the county clerk at the courthouse has an absolute wealth of information concerning architects and engineers and potential clients. Depending on how open the access to these records is and on the building requirements of your particular courthouse, you should be able to find information concerning current building projects—who the architects/engineers are, the owner of the project, and so on. Visit your county courthouse no less than once a month, preferably as often as once each week, to secure as much information from these public records as you possibly can. Other information available at the courthouse concerns newly formed businesses. In some states you are required to register any time you open a business, even if you are not required to be licensed by the state. These are public records. Often you will find that an A/E firm is doing business as another firm. What is important is the information that the developer or the A/E firm is required to provide when issuing this filing. Each state and county in the United States differs in its requirements: some require more information and some less.

In some cities and states, whenever requests for bids go out and someone is awarded a contract, this information is also published as a matter of public record in the county clerk's office or city hall. It may include a published overhead rate, the number of employees, billing rate, and so forth. Occasionally the bids not awarded the contract are also published. There is no way we can tell you about all the information that may be available at your local clerk's office. The point is, you should use the public records as much as you can. They are public, open to anyone, and it is up to you to avail yourself of them. Once you have found the information you are interested in, review it on a periodic basis.

TECHNIQUE #5: READ THE SIGNS

We know that as you drive through your city, out of curiosity you notice signs on new buildings and projects going up. These state who the architects are, who the engineers are, who the developers are, and like information. If you are an architect who wishes to find out about another architect, or an engineer about another engineer, here are a few of the easiest things to do:

1. Who is doing what project? You can add this to your data base of A/E firms on projects being done.
2. Call the opposite counterpart. For example, if you are an engineer wishing to know about another engineer, call the architectural firm on that project, and indicate that you are interested in doing a joint venture with the engineer working

on the project and would appreciate a reference. Then ask your questions.

The point is to gather as much information as you possibly can. Find out not only what the strengths of your competitors are, but also where their weaknesses lie.

TECHNIQUE #6: CALL THE LANDLORD

The A/E firm that you are interested in may be in an office building. It is easy to call the management of that building to inquire about office space. This way you can find out how much the rents are. As you talk further, simply mention that you have noticed that a certain firm is in the building and that you too are an A/E firm. Find out how long the firm has been in that location, whether there are other architects or engineers in that building, and so on.

Generally, the more rent paid and space owned by an architectural or engineering firm, the higher its overhead rate. Some of the information you will get will be like this—bits and pieces that you must put together in order to make an educated guess.

Concerning the overhead rate, which is a very important piece of information, you can first compute your own overhead rate and draw a correlation of that rate to a per employee cost of rental space. For example, if your rental cost is $1,500.00 a month and you have 8 employees, your cost per employee for rent would be $187.50. (You have previously computed that your overhead rate is 165 percent.) Now let us say that a firm in competition with you pays a rent of $2,700.00 a month and that this firm has 13 employees. Its per employee rental rate is $207.69. Now divide your cost per employee ($187.50) into the other firm's ($207.69) to see what percentage more that firm is paying than you are. The answer is 1.11, which means that their cost is 11 percent higher than yours.

What we have found is that for a given area you can get a conservative estimate by dividing this number by 2 and applying that increase to your overhead rate to arrive at an approximation of what the other firm's overhead rate is. In this case you would divide 11 by 2, which equals 5.5 (rounded off to 6.0). You would then take your overhead rate of 165 percent and increase it by 6 percent. Their overhead rate would be approximately 175 percent.

Needless to say, this is a very rough guess, since, as you know, there are more indirect costs that affect overhead. The biggest is the ratio of direct time to total time or, better stated, how much in direct dollars of fixed labor is being applied to the direct expenditure section as opposed to indirect labor amounts. That is why, to stay on the conservative side, we take only half of the increase per employee for rent and assume that this adjustment will account for additional overhead factors. (The assumption is that with the additional overhead and additional employees, your competitor is at least as efficient as your firm, if not more so.) Obviously, the same general formula would hold true if your rent per employee was more than that of your competition's. You would first find out how much less percentagewise it was, divide by 2, and subtract that percentage from your overhead rate to get an approximation of the overhead rate of your competition.

As you can see from the techniques described above, a wealth of information can be gathered about your competitors. As we said at the beginning of this chapter, do not feel compelled to use any of these techniques. Use only the ones that you personally feel comfortable with. As you begin to use the various techniques listed above, however, you may wish to phase in others. The more information you can secure about a competitor, the better off you will be in competing for projects within your field.

Advertising

As discussed in previous chapters, the purpose of advertising is to let your potential clients know who you are, what your services are, and what you can do for them. Advertising facilitates the step that follows, which is contact with the client. It has only one major objective: to meet the client. It is only when you meet the client that you have even the slightest possibility of providing service to that client.

In this chapter we are going to discuss three primary media of advertising that have been effective in marketing A/E services: direct mail, telemarketing, and print media.

DIRECT MAIL

Before we begin with the actual content of direct mail, let us first talk a little about the mechanics of using this medium. One of the reasons that direct mail is so effective is that the number of potential clients you may serve is limited. If you were selling cars, soap, televisions, or any other consumer goods, the cost of direct mail would be absolutely prohibitive, especially if that cost was measured in terms of the percentage of total potential clients. If you take a small city of 500,000 and assume that your potential clients number 300,000, then even if you could get the cost of the direct mail down to 50¢ per item, it would cost you $150,000 to reach each of these clients one time. Even a large A/E firm would totally exhaust its entire advertising budget if this were its potential client base.

For the same reason, those firms with smaller potential client bases find direct mail extremely effective. If you number your entire client base at 3,000, you could use some of the other media and never reach all of them. Direct mail gives you the opportunity with each mailing to reach 100 percent of your entire potential client base at a very reasonable cost. It also adds a certain personal touch because you are willing to invest in reaching each one of your clients.

One of the first questions you are going to have to answer is how the mailing is going to be delivered to your clients. This seems like a very elementary issue, and the answer seems obvious. Mail it! The real question is whether to use third-class or first-class mail. Bulk mail, as third-class mail is called, costs approximately 50 percent of what first-class costs. There are two main disadvantages of bulk mail. First, it is much slower than first-class mail. Second, since the recipient usually considers bulk mail to be junk mail, you run the risk that your mail will not even be opened. On the other hand, you can send twice as many mailers for the same budget amount.

We have had varying degrees of success with bulk mail as far as speed of delivery is concerned. Letters sent locally using bulk mail are sometimes delivered in the same amount of time as first-class mail is: usually one or two days. By the same token, if you are mailing out of city or state, bulk mail can take as long as one to two weeks for delivery. For our purposes, however, we do not consider the time of delivery to be a significant handicap considering the cost savings of a bulk mailer. One technique we use whenever we do a mailer is to mail one of the items to ourselves, using a home address. This gives us some indication of when the piece was delivered.

Naturally, if you are sending an initial congratulatory letter, you should use first-class postage because the announcement in the newspaper is already one to two months after the fact and any further delay would reduce the impact of such a letter.

Assuming that you have paid for the privilege, one thing that bulk mail allows you to do is to have a preprinted imprint on the envelope. Basically this is a notice that says postage has been paid for by your mailing permit (number imprinted on the envelope). What this means is that if you are sending out 3,000 items, you do not have to lick 3,000 stamps. Just have your permit stamp printed on the envelope ahead of time. Of course this unmistakably marks your mailing as bulk mail.

The bulk mail stamp is another option. There is no increased cost, except your time and effort, since you must affix the stamps to your letters. These stamps are not grotesquely ugly nor appreciably different from first-class stamps, and they have one primary advantage: the stamp itself says bulk mail, but unless you look closely, all you see is an envelope with a stamp on it. With all the unique postage stamps the United States government has been issuing in recent years, one strange-looking stamp looks no different from another strange-looking stamp. By using these stamps, chances are you might avoid the stigma of junk mail.

If you have ever folded, stuffed, and sealed 3,000 envelopes, however, you know that the very last thing you want to do next is affix 3,000 stamps. We have a general rule: If our bulk mailing is 500 to 600, we use a bulk mail stamp, if our mailing is in the thousands, we will accept the lesser effectiveness and use the imprint.

The next item that needs to be considered is the envelope that the mailing goes into. There are, of course, ways to avoid having to lick envelopes and stuff mailers. Some people use fold-overs with a staple through them and the address printed on the outside. There is nothing that is going to identify your mailing as junk mail quicker than this method. We recommend that all mailings be sent in a clean envelope with your letterhead/logo printed as the return address, just as any other first-class letter to a client would be. This takes a bit of time and is a little more expensive, but we feel it is much more effective and well worth the effort. This does not mean that you should use your most expensive envelopes and matching letterhead. Have less expensive envelopes printed with your logo and return address in the upper left corner.

One of the biggest problems with mass mailings, as we have mentioned, is that once they are identified as being bulk mail, they are often disregarded or thrown into the trash unopened. There are tricks many companies use to fool the consumer into thinking a bulk mail piece is important. Some of them have "Time Sensitive Material Inside—Open Immediately" printed on the outside of the envelope itself; others say "Confidential." Then there are the ones that indicate you have won something. We have even seen mass mailings that purposely use brown envelopes in an attempt to look like Internal Revenue Service or other governmental agency correspondence; the last thing anyone is going to do is throw one of those in the trash can unopened. Still others have cellophane window envelopes partially revealing a letter that looks like a check saying "Pay to the order of . . ." Please avoid these tricks. They may indeed get your material opened, but the resentment they engender often makes them useless.

One other technique is sending the mailer out in a plain white envelope with no logo or letterhead. The idea is, if there is no return address on the envelope, it will be opened. There is one proviso: the address must be hand written. If you use this technique with mailing labels, you are wasting your time.

Your next concern is addressing the envelope. If you are using a computer, there are several ways that the envelope can be addressed. The most common method is the use of mailing labels. Computers are very adept at producing these. They are peel-off adhesives on tractor-feed that moves through your computer printer, which produces your labels directly from your data base. Actually, this does give the appearance of a mass mailer. However, there are two types of labels: plain white and transparent. Transparent labels tend to look more like they were typed on the envelope.

Some printers are capable of feeding envelopes on tractor-feed with laser cuts so that no telltale perforations on the envelope can be detected. If you are going to go to the expense of using this technique, be sure you use a letter-quality daisy-wheel printer. If you use a dot-matrix printer, you might as well go ahead and use the mailing labels since no matter how good you think the print quality of your dot-matrix is, most people can tell when something came off of a dot-matrix printer. Also, make sure that your data base is in both upper and lower case. One of the surest signs that a mailing list has come off a computer is an address in all capital letters. If you are using one of the laser-type printers that are on the market today, you may have varying degrees of success feeding actual envelopes through. An alternative to using printed labels might be to type the address yourself.

You have two choices for the printed material that goes inside the envelope: a personalized mailmerge original or bulk-printed copy. The difference is that mailmerge permits you to write a personalized letter using variables such as the contact person's name and inside address, then sprinkle the name of the company throughout the material itself. Thus you have an individual letter printed on your computer with the personalized name, address, and company name on each individual letter. The alternative is to do one generic letter, making no references to any particular company, then to take it down to your local quick print shop and have as many copies as you need printed. Naturally the latter is the least expensive and the easiest to do.

If you decide to bypass mailmerge and still maintain a letter format, you will have to deal with the signature. Though it is tempting to just sign one letter and have the signature reproduced by your print shop, you should never use a facsimile of a signature. Make sure the letter is signed by a person. This goes for each item mailed. Naturally, it need not be the same person signing all 3,000 letters. Everyone in your office can sign 100 letters. No one is going to match the signatures. Make sure that you sign the letters in ink that is a color different from the print. There is no reason to go to the trouble of signing all the letters individually in black ink and have them look like printer-reproduced signatures. Use blue, green, red, or any distinctive color that you feel is appropriate. If your client has to look closely to see whether or not you actually signed his letter, you lose the impact.

Let us look again at the purposes of mailers:

1. They get potential clients to call. This is absolutely essential. You want them to pick up the phone and to call you. Only then will you be able to talk with them and arrange a time that you can meet them in person. This is the first step in getting to know the potential client.
2. Potential clients may save this mailer and all future mailers for future reference. Not everybody builds a project tomorrow; not everyone has a use for your services today. But someday, when this potential client is in need of an architect or engineer, he may refer to the file that the firm has kept over the months or years. Your desired goal is for the client to pick up the file and see your name 15 or 20 times. Then he will call you.
3. They make follow-up easier. No one likes cold-calling. If you need to have a reason to call, this gives you an easy excuse: You are following up on the letter you sent them.

TYPE OF MAILERS

There are various types of mailers and each has a different purpose. The first type is the congratulatory letter. This will go to your general contacts. It can also go to your clients when you have a reason to congratulate them. Actively look for a reason. Comb the newspapers; look for announcements they have made.

Find some reason to send them a letter to congratulate them on an achievement. Remember: Do not send these letters bulk mail. As a rule you will not have enough of them to qualify for bulk mailing, but that is not the point. A congratulatory letter needs to be first-class and so should be mailed first-class.

Another type of mailer is the letter of introduction (this could be combined with a congratulatory letter if the situation arises). This probably should be the very first mailer you send out to each of your potential clients. It is simply a letter in which you introduce yourself, your firm, what you do, why you feel you can do it better than your competitor, and specifically what you feel you can do for this potential client. Feel free to brag about your accomplishments and completed projects, and be a name dropper if your existing clients will be meaningful to the recipient. Stress that you are there to serve the potential client and that if there is anything you can do for him in the future, he should call you.

Once you have sent out an introductory letter to each of your clients, future correspondence should be in the form of the advertising letter. All of the advertising letters you send out should have the same components: an introduction telling the client what the letter is about, who you are, what you do, and why you are writing the letter. The most effective advertising letter will always have some type of free offer. Naturally this should be a professional offer and should require no action by or cost to the potential client other than telephoning to ask for it. The offer might be a free report on the economic performance of your city, a survey you wish to share, or anything else interesting enough to make the client call you and request it. Under no circumstances should the free offer be a come-on, nor should the client feel tricked because after receiving it he must purchase something else to use it.

Remember there is one, and only one, reason for making this offer and sending out the letter: to entice the client to call you so that you will have the opportunity to speak with him and to follow up at a future time. The final component of the letter should be an invitation to call for the free offer. Try to make the invitation as painless and easy (nonthreatening) for the client as possible. Remember that the client wants to hide from you. He wants to remain as anonymous as possible. It is the free offer that can make him visible to you.

The next type of mailer is the questionnaire. Basically the questionnaire is a written survey that requests the client to fill in some information and return it to you. It is your questionnaire, so feel free to ask anything you want. Remember, you are not necessarily attempting to elicit information for your data base (as was the case with the questionnaire you sent to your competitor). What you want here is an open invitation to call the client after you receive the completed questionnaire and talk further with him about his answers. You might ask him about the types of projects he is involved in, what he likes about the current A/E firms he works with, and whether he has been dissatisfied with A/E firms in the past and why. You might make this in the form of a checklist.

There are two essential questions to include on the questionnaire for the potential client to answer:

1. How do you feel about the cost of A/E services?
2. How do you feel about projects that are not completed on time?

The reason you want to include these two specific questions is that although no developer on the face of the earth is going to say he feels that A/E services are too low or that he would prefer his projects be completed late, his answers will give you the opportunity to follow up. You can call the developer to sympathize with him about high prices and to suggest that maybe by working together on a future project you can correct some of the problems he has had in the past.

The questionnaire offers the perfect vehicle for another type of telephone follow-up. It gives you the opportunity to call your potential client to ask whether he received the questionnaire and, possibly, if he has not had a chance to fill it out, whether he could take a few moments to answer some questions on the telephone.

The last type of mailer is the newsletter. This is a cross between direct advertising and public relations. When used as advertising, the newsletter should always include something to entice the user to pick up the phone and ask for more information. It can be information you have at your disposal that was not complete at press time and that you would be happy to send upon request. Or it might leave some unanswered questions that you offer to discuss with readers if they give you a call.

If you are going to do a newsletter, make sure you include useful and timely information in each and every issue. The reader must never feel that he has been tricked into reading an advertisement. Even if you get no responses, you should not feel that the newsletter is a waste of time, money, and effort. It simply means that it is not advertising but public relations and should be in the public relations budget.

Finally, you might consider sending out an advertising letter offering a free subscription to your newsletter. All the potential client needs to do is call and sign up. Then when he gets the newsletter, there will be other free offers, and so on, and so on. This is called nesting offers within offers.

TELEMARKETING

The purpose of telemarketing is to make direct contact with the potential client; it is not to sell A/E services over the phone. You have already used telephone surveys to gain information about both potential clients and your competitors, so you are familiar with telephone techniques. A few hints, however, follow.

To begin, simply pick up the telephone, call the potential client, and ask for an appointment. Either you will get one or you will not. Remember, the purpose is not to sell a major office complex or a set of plans; it is to give you the opportunity to meet potential clients.

If you do not feel you can pick up the phone and ask for an appointment with an individual, try calling to follow up on an offer you have made and ask permission to send whatever it was you were offering. On the other hand, if the potential client has not received the mailer making the offer, apologize, confirm his address, tell him about the offer, and ask permission to send it.

In fact, any time you make an offer, regardless of what it is or why it was sent, you should follow up with a telephone call. Remember: The reason for sending out the advertising letter in the first place was to entice the client to call you and to give you an excuse to call him at a future time to discuss his needs in detail in order to develop a proposal to serve those needs.

Needless to say, you have been building quite a diverse data base of potential clients. Not every potential client is necessarily going to be interested in a report that you have put together on the potential growth of the community in single-family housing, or on the cost increases of certain products. Schools, for example, might be interested in a report on new housing subdivisions and an increase in building permits in their particular school district. On the other hand, developers might be interested in a report concerning a survey you have conducted on office vacancy. The point is that you should have more than one mailer, as well as more than one free offer, not simply a mass mailer to everyone in your data base. You should use a client code to zero in on which clients to send which mailers. Tailor each mailer to one particular industry and the unique services that you can provide that industry.

When doing any type of direct mail advertising, you should keep meticulous records on each mailer that is sent out, including when it was mailed and to which type of client, and what the general response to the mailer was (attitude, reception, and number of direct responses). In this way, over a period of time you will be able to fine tune your mailings to the types of things that work in your particular area with a particular type of client.

PRINT ADVERTISING

Dollar for dollar, print advertising is not as effective as direct mail when a potential client base is limited, as is the case with an A/E firm. Therefore print advertising should be used sparingly. If it is used, it should be targeted to a general group. For example, there is absolutely no reason to place an ad in *People* magazine or in *TV Guide* or possibly even in your local newspaper. Although you may reach a vast number of people, you will not have targeted your audience at all. Some good media for print advertising include publications put out by your local Chamber of Commerce (magazine or newspaper form), magazines or trade journals targeted at builders or developers, or any industry-specific magazine your potential client might read.

Although they are in the public relations category, you should consider taking out ads in your local school publications. These can be yearbooks, football programs, or anything that the students sell advertising for in order to raise money. This is public relations because it probably will not result in a new project for your firm, but the school board appreciates such support and does tend to remember it.

BUDGETING YOUR ADVERTISING DOLLAR

Before we leave this chapter on advertising, let us review once again exactly how you should be computing your advertising dollars. First ad up your fee and reimbursable revenue and then subtract all direct expenses except direct labor. This should be the revenue upon which your advertising budget is based. Most advertising budgets equal approximately 5 to 10 percent of this figure; they absolutely should not fall below 3 percent. Whatever your advertising budget is, make sure that a minimum of 60 percent is available for direct advertising. When you look at these figures you may decide you cannot afford to do this kind of advertising, but the truth is you cannot afford not to.

Public Relations

Public relations is probably what you do best if your firm is doing any marketing at all. As we pointed out previously, probably 90 percent of your current marketing activities fall in this category. Keep in mind, however, that although public relations is an important part of marketing, indeed an essential one, there is more to marketing than just public relations. The point is that you must balance the priorities of your marketing budget, of which public relations plays just one part.

With this said, let us go on to objectives of public relations. These are threefold:

1. To enhance your image to your clients
2. To create name recognition
3. To foster professional credibility

As we mentioned in the chapter on selling, people buy a thing because of emotions and then rationalize that purchase through reason. They also have a natural desire to buy the best. In the case of A/E services, people want others to know that they have engaged the best, most qualified, and most respectable firm in the industry. This is where image comes in.

The purpose of advertising is to let people know who you are and what you can do for them. The purpose of public relations is to reinforce that advertising and to make people believe it.

THE BROCHURE

Every A/E firm should have a good brochure. We are not talking about a $50,000 masterpiece nor are we referring to the proposal. This brochure should basically tell the story of your firm: who the people are, their credentials, what some of your more impressive projects have been, and so forth.

The brochure should have a professional quality to it; it should not look like it was done on your duplicating machine. It should be professionally typeset, possibly with photographic images or graphics. You want to spend ample money on your brochure because this is the first image that a potential client will have of you and your firm. At the same time, your budget needs to be reasonable (remember that all your public relations efforts should not exceed 30 percent of your marketing budget). The problem with many brochures in the A/E industry is that they are so overdone and overly expensive that the A/E firm does not want to give them out to potential clients until they are at the proposal stage.

Your brochure should not be too large. It should be easily mailable, along with all of the other information that you will be sending a potential client. Give out your brochure freely. They do absolutely no good sitting in your supply closet. Make sure you include a copy of your brochure with every free offer you send to a potential client. Send brochures with your press announcements. In fact, you should hand out brochures almost as freely as you now hand out business cards. You want your potential clients, general contacts, and the public not only to be impressed by your brochure but to be absolutely inundated with information on the work you have done.

GENERAL CLUBS

We are not talking about service organizations, such as the Kiwanis or Rotary Club, in this section. We are referring to dinner clubs, country clubs, and so on, where the purpose of joining is to make professional contacts that eventually could lead to projects and other business activities.

Choose your club carefully. If there is a club you simply want to belong to and you put it into your marketing budget for the purpose of expensing it on your general ledger, fully realizing that this expense is not a part of your marketing effort, fine. If, on the other hand, you want to make your membership meaningful, choose your club very wisely and make sure you know the current membership of the club before you join.

Supposedly the club offers you a place to entertain potential clients, but any fine restaurant within your city would do just as well. On the other hand, potential clients may belong to that club and you might want to join for the actual business contacts. Otherwise the cost of a club membership should be evaluated alongside other expenditures within the limitations of your public relations budget.

SERVICE ORGANIZATIONS

Service organizations belong in an entirely different category. The service organization does not require a large membership fee or an ongoing large expenditure, as does a private club membership. At the same time it affords various opportunities for public relations.

For one thing, many of your potential clients may also be members of this same service organization. Thus membership often affords an opportunity to meet these individuals and network extensively.

Most service organizations perform true community services and you might want to join simply because you want to do work that will benefit your local community. Beyond that, extensive activity in service organizations provides a vehicle for good publicity for you and your firm, high visibility, and an opportunity to enhance name recognition. Service organizations also enable you to donate the services of your firm on community projects, again enhancing name recognition.

Remember when budgeting for community involvement and service organizations that the costs can be extensive, in terms of both dollars and time.

THE PRINT MEDIA

In the chapter on advertising, we talked very briefly about print advertising and mentioned that it can be used in a variety of ways. If you use print advertising to make an offer or to elicit a response from a potential client, that is advertising. If, on the other hand, the advertisement is primarily an announcement, it generally falls into the category of public relations. There is nothing wrong with this because print advertising is a very important component of public relations (in fact, we feel that print advertising belongs more in the field of public relations than it does in direct advertising). We offer one word of advice: Since you are spending money, always attempt to arrange a quid pro quo editorial trade-off in exchange for your advertising business. In that way your advertisement, which is primarily for the purpose of public relations, reinforces the editorial article or comment in the publication, which is actually what is doing the selling for you. Try to budget your scarce print advertising dollars for use in only those publications that offer you this kind of support.

Articles and News Releases

There is a third data base that we would like you to create: news publications. All that is required for this data base is names and addresses because you will be using it simply to produce mailing labels.

One of the best types of advertising is free advertising. The reason free advertising is the best is not simply because the cost is right, but because it comes in the form of editorial comments about you.

Most people have a natural reluctance to believe the statements made in advertisements. On the other hand, if the same statements appear in an editorial, for example, people are more willing to accept them as fact. Therefore, editorial comments or news releases published in magazines and newspapers can be extremely advantageous in producing the kind of image, name recognition, and credibility you are looking for in your public relations efforts.

On the flip side of the coin, newspapers and other publications are constantly looking for public interest announcements and articles to act as fillers; they are also often willing to make all kinds of arrangements to provide you with this editorial space in return for the promise of future advertising. Needless to say, you do not want, nor can you afford, to advertise in every magazine and periodical that will simply allot you editorial space. What you should do is select for extensive advertising those publications that will do you the most good, naturally in return for additional editorial comments.

Having editorial comments and write-ups about your firm in various publications is basically a matter of numbers. It should not take much time to do some research on publications suitable to your particular area and to enter their names and addresses in your data base (we recommend that you have at least 50). You should then send information to these on a regular basis.

Before most publications will do a write-up on you or publish your news releases, they generally require something called a fact sheet. Basically this consists of some directory information on your firm, such as name, address, telephone number, date founded, principal owners, and contact person. In addition, you should include a brief description of who you are and what you do. This should not be too long—usually no more than two pages. It should be written in a form that makes it easy for the publisher to lift portions out in their entirety to use with very little editing in an article. Actually, this is your goal. You would like nothing better than for the publication to reproduce your fact sheet in an editorial comment concerning your firm. The fact sheet also serves another purpose. When you send out a press release to the various publications, the first thing they will do is check to see if they have a fact sheet on file in order to ascertain what type of company yours is. It is perfectly acceptable to send a fact sheet along with your first news release or article.

Actually, it is easier to have your news releases published than it is to have full-fledged articles written about you. In fact most publications have an entire section for new product announcements, new releases, and items of interest about the business community for the areas that they serve.

As an absolute minimal goal, you should strive for at least one news release to each of the publications on your list once a month (you could send out something to everyone on the list every other week, if you wish). What do you put into these releases? That is the easiest part. Include news about any new contracts you have signed, individuals that have recently joined your firm, promotions of individuals within your firm, new services that you are offering to the public, and so on. Try to make these appear as newsworthy as possible. If you are coming out with a new service or wish to publicize an existing one that you provide to your clients, try to find something unique about this service. The following is an example: "Due to a recently acquired CAD system, XYZ Architectural Company can now better service its clients not only in speed and efficiency, but also at a more reasonable fee structure." The object is to get your name published in as many different areas as possible. A new focus for each announcement is helpful, with each announcement highlighting a different service of your firm.

Professional Journals

The next area of public relations we want to discuss has to do primarily with professional journals, which publish more specialized types of articles. You should consider writing these types of articles, but be sure your topic is of interest to your peers. Write an article at least once each month and submit it to the various professional publications to which you subscribe. Do not get discouraged. Eventually one of these will be accepted for publication; all it takes is persistence. The object of this exercise is not only to increase your name recognition and prestige, but also to add to your firm's credibility. You can use the fact that you have been published in professional journals as part of your public relations efforts.

You should also consider writing articles for more general publications. Submit these on a regular basis along with any press releases you have prepared. These articles should be of interest to the average reader and should therefore be "popular" in nature.

SOCIAL GATHERINGS

If you are an architect or an engineer, this is the type of public relations you already do best and it probably has been your greatest marketing effort. We are referring to social gatherings. These could be a cocktail party, Christmas party, seminar meeting, or any gathering where possible business contacts may be made and business cards exchanged. Many local Chambers of Commerce sponsor such meetings as business mixers. These are even advertised as being held for the expressed purpose of making business contacts. They always include in their invitation, "Bring plenty of business cards." There is absolutely nothing wrong with these types of meetings. In fact, they can provide a wealth of new contacts and possibilities for future business. Unfortunately, most architects and engineers do not have the slightest idea of how to handle these meetings correctly. They take plenty of business cards and hand them all out in one evening. They get bogged down in a discussion, or maybe even talk a little business. So far they have done everything wrong.

The purpose of such meetings is to make contacts, not to conduct business. You are at a disadvantage since you do not control the environment or the presentation, and if you meet an individual and hand him or her your card, what have you got? Absolutely nothing.

The first thing we want you to do is leave all of your business cards at home. When you give a business card to a general contact or even to a potential client, where do you think that card goes? Do you really think that he is going to give you a call the next morning? The best you can hope for is that your card will land in a desk drawer. What probably will happen to it is that either it will go to the laundry in his pocket or it will be thrown out.

When you are at these gatherings, you should not be giving out business cards—you should be collecting them. As you talk to people, ask them for their card. If they ask you for a card, politely say, "I'm sorry, I don't know what I was thinking of. I left mine at home (or back at the office), but may I have your card?" Instead of cards, always bring a small, pocket-sized writing tablet in case others there have read this book and have also left their business cards at home. Simply take out the tablet and have them write their name, address, and telephone number on one of the pages. Naturally, if they insist that they want your name and address, be courteous and write it down for them. You are not trying to hide and you really do not care whether they have your business cards or not. The purpose of this meeting is for you to get theirs. Look at it from this perspective: If they give you their business card or they write down their name, address, and telephone number, what have they said to you? *Call me!* This is an open invitation to pick up the phone the next day and set an appointment. If all you do is hand them a card, you will probably never hear from them again.

As you can see, most of the items we have discussed thus far really have not been costly. They basically consist of writing articles, sending news announcements, going to special get-togethers, and becoming involved in community services. These are activities intended to make your name well known and enhance your image and professional credibility.

Your approach to public relations, however, should not be haphazard. It requires dedicated effort, must be organized and controlled, and not left strictly to chance. You must compile your mailing list of publications. You must compose and send out your press announcements on a regular basis. You must budget and spend the time in order to take leadership roles in service organizations. You must do the research necessary to write the articles for publications and professional journals. All of these things are necessary if your direct advertising and the contacts you are going to make are to prove fruitful. Remember that everyone wants to be associated with the best. You can project this image only with diligent effort, perseverance, and consistent exposure.

Selling

Earlier in this part, we discussed the statement, "I am not a salesman." Most of you, if you are honest with yourselves, would probably agree with this. Unfortunately, one of the things that our schools and colleges do not teach, and even grossly ignore, is selling. There is no such thing as the "born salesman." Selling is a skill, and like any other skill, it must be learned.

The problem is that when you were in college learning your profession, chances are nobody ever told you that you were going to have to sell something. When you graduated from college and went to work for someone else, possibly in another A/E firm, you were sheltered from this world as you engaged in your professional activities. You probably never even stopped to think that someone had to sell those services so that your salary could be paid. When you opened your own business, possibly you were lucky enough to bring some clients with you and some nice contracts to get you started. But we have seen firms go into business absolutely cold turkey, without one existing client. It is scary to sit in a new office, looking around at all the trappings of success, without one idea of where your first client is going to come from. It is even scarier after a year in the business, when bills are mounting up, you have salaries that must be paid, utilization rates are dropping, and you are moaning about the state of the economy. Unfortunately, the term *sales* conjures up so many negative visions and instills such fear in the hearts of so many individuals that it is hard for most of us to admit that when we go into business for ourselves, we must sell in order to eat.

If you think of salesmen as people who make you buy things you do not want, the first thing you will have to do is change your concept of what a salesman does. A salesman is simply an individual who helps a potential client make a decision that is in that client's best interest.

Many people have a difficult time making a decision, so you can expect that it will not be easy for your clients to make a decision regarding the services you have to offer. They are afraid of making the wrong decision and they need your help and guidance. You get paid as much for helping and guiding them into the decisions that are necessary to complete their projects as you do for the technical aspects of your job.

The problem is that if you are like most A/E professionals, you do not know the first thing about selling. You are probably just winging it, totally unprepared. The purpose of this chapter is to acquaint you with an organized method of selling your services to your particular client in a professional manner. Our goal is to help you begin to understand what is necessary so that you can help your clients.

Let us start by looking at the five essential steps in the selling process.

PROSPECTING

Although we went into some detail on prospecting earlier in this part, we purposely did not use this word to keep from scaring you off. *Prospecting* is a term for finding and ferreting out potential clients. This first step in the selling process involves finding out who your potential clients are, making a list of them, and then making an initial contact with them by mail, telephone, and other forms of direct advertising. Even in what might be considered retail sales, where it looks as though the client comes to you, if someone did not prospect through effective media advertising, nobody would come into the store.

MEETING PEOPLE

Unless you are selling strictly by mail, there are very few projects that you will ever get without meeting the people involved. This is vital. Selling is a numbers game. You are not going to sell 100 percent of the prospects that you meet; not everyone you meet will be qualified for the services that you have to offer. No matter how hard you try, there will sometimes be conditions that prevent you from guiding even qualified individuals to a decision that is in their best interest. Therefore you can only hope to sell a certain percentage of the people you meet. This percentage differs for each industry, service, profession, and product. Even people within the same profession may have a different percentage of success. It is hoped that this chapter will help you increase those percentages, but it is still a numbers game. Until you can increase the percentage of sales made, there is only one other surefire way to increase the number of sales. Meet more people. It is a proven fact that the more people you meet, the more sales you will make in absolute numbers.

Let us say for the sake of argument that you make one sale and get one contract with a profit of $35,000 for your company for every 50 qualified prospective clients that you meet. All you have to do is meet one more potential client than you are currently meeting per week for the next year and you will have increased your annual income by $35,000 for that year.

QUALIFICATION

You could go to a prospective client's office, make the best presentation the client has ever seen, thrill him with your image and professional credentials, get him to agree with you on the quality and type of services you can perform, and offer him reasonable fees for extraordinary service. But unless that client has a need for your services, there is no way you are going to reach a contract. Qualification is one of the most important aspects of selling and, quite honestly, it is one of the most overlooked and misunderstood.

When the average individual thinks of qualification, the first thing that crosses his mind is the process of qualifying for a loan or for the purchase of real estate. Many of the aspects that are involved in the purchase of real estate are part of the qualification sequence, but they are not all of it and are not the entire purpose. You have heard real estate agents tell you that you qualify for a house or a loan up to a certain amount. What they are doing in their own mind is deciding what to show you. Obviously if your income qualifies you for no more than a $120,000 house, it would be a waste of both your and the real estate agent's time to show you a house in the $300,000 range. They are beginning the qualification sequence so they can help you make a decision that is right for you.

Qualification is not just for finding out how much the client can afford to spend; it also serves other essential purposes. Before you can sell anything to a client, you, as a professional, must decide what you are going to sell that client. This might sound like a silly statement, but until you make up your own mind about what the client needs and what you are going to sell him, you will never sell him anything. The client may buy, but it will be in spite of you, not because of you. Remember, you are a professional in your field of expertise. If your client knew how to do schematics, design, or any of the other professional services that you are prepared to offer him, he would not need you. Therefore it is your responsibility as the professional to make many of the important decisions for the client.

Of course you should not go about it blindly. This is one of the purposes of qualification. You must ask questions to find out what the client wants, what he needs, and what he is interested in. You must probe to get at the true answers because unless you understand what the client really wants, you cannot make a professional decision about what will satisfy him.

If you are doing this now, chances are you are doing it haphazardly in your general discussions with the client concerning a potential project. Many times you will simply put together some predesign work and give an estimate/proposal. This is part of it. What you are finding out is the scope of the project.

The first bit of information you need to know is what the client is doing currently. What firms is he using now or has he used in the past? If you have done your homework properly, you will already have the answers to these questions and can approximate what the client has been paying in the past for A/E services as well as have an idea of the quality and reputation of the firms.

The next thing you need to know is which services was the client most pleased with. What is it he liked most about the firms he has used in the past. Needless to say, the answers will give you an indication of what his desires are concerning services and what he expects from you. Naturally you are going to emphasize those benefits that the client has shown a willingness to accept, but the main thing you need to find out is where the company would like to see improvement in the services provided. This lets you know where the client's sore spots are and what he is dissatisfied with. Being forewarned in this area can help tremendously.

One further qualification question you must ask is who will make the final decision concerning this project. We cannot begin to tell you how many times firms make full presentations only to be told that someone else will make the decision. If you know this ahead of time, you will know that you should make only a partial presentation and that the closings you do will not be for the contract but for the opportunity to make a full presentation to the decision makers. This is absolutely critical, especially if you are working with governmental or highly bureaucratic organizations.

The selling of A/E services generally requires more than one meeting with a potential client before the details and commitment of a contract are established. This gives you the opportunity to test the waters for the type of services that you are going to be providing to the client and also the budgeted fee involved. Once you have made the decision on the type of services the client needs, it is up to you to help the client with the decision that these are the services he needs to pursue. The amount of money the client is going to spend for the A/E services provided also has to be determined by you and guided to a successful conclusion. One method of accomplishing this is known as the triplicate of choice, for service and for price.

Basically the way the triplicate of choice for service works is that you take three possibilities, each of which are going to have different cost factors involved due to the scope and sophistication of the services being provided. You present these with the one you would like the client to choose positioned in the middle. The psychology behind this is very simple. Most people would prefer to be neither too extravagant nor too cheap, and they tend, when given an obvious small, medium, or large choice, to almost always choose the medium.

Once the triplicate of choice for service has been established, begin with a triplicate of choice for price in order to find out approximately how much the client can afford to pay for the services. By presenting the proposals in rough figures (and, of course, this will not be your actual proposal for the cost of your professional services), you can get an idea of the potential client's budget range. You indicate that, for these services, some of your clients tend to budget, a figure around ______ (name a number about 20 to 30 percent higher than the figure would be for what they have chosen in the triplicate of choice for service). Following that, you mention that there are those of your clients that are fortunate enough to be able to afford ______ (name a figure still higher). Also mention that you have clients on a limited budget who must carefully watch their expenditures on a project and be very conservative; they tend to budget _____ (name a figure just slightly higher than the approximate professional fees that you are going to propose for the middle item in the triplicate of choice for service).

The psychology behind this is primarily a defense mechanism. Most people, when presented with a triplicate of choice for services, will tend to choose the middle one since usually there is no price tag attached to their choice. When this is tactfully followed by a triplicate of choice for price, a general defense mechanism comes into play and they equate the cost of the three in the triplicate of choice for service with the triplicate of choice for price. In order to defend themselves in what is obviously the closing sequence, they will say that they are on a limited budget, have to watch everything very carefully, and fall into the lesser cost category. Since you have planned this well, the lesser price category falls somewhere above what you are going to propose for the middle choice. Meanwhile the client comes up with the excuse that he cannot afford the price because what he really wants is the middle selection at the lower price. Everything naturally falls into place when he finds that the proposal comes in lower than what he said his firm was willing to pay for what he said the firm wanted.

The final hook in the triplicate of choice for service and price is a minor closing sequence in which you ask once again if, on the condition that you get him the services you have agreed upon for the price he has agreed his firm can afford, his firm is in a position to proceed with the project. You are not discussing if the client is going to engage your services; now you are simply talking money. Once it can be reduced to money, the client has bought.

PRESENTATION

The next item in the sales sequence is the presentation. Unfortunately, some people attempt to wing it when they first meet a client. They put absolutely no preparation into what they are going to say, what they are going to do, what the goal of the meeting is, or what they hope to accomplish. Once they have the appointment, they just show up and start talking.

A professional, on the other hand, preplans everything, and that is what you must do for every meeting with potential clients throughout the sales process. Write it down. Make a list of the benefits that have been accepted in a previous discussion. Make a list of the benefits that you think they will accept. List what the anticipated objections are. Make a list of the materials that you are going to use: your brochure, information concerning similar projects that you have done, or audiovisual materials. Write out similar-situation stories. If a client comes up with reasons why he does not want to proceed or if he seems hesitant, to put him at ease you should have some stories concerning other clients that were in a similar situation and how they resolved it.

Make a list of items of personal interest that you might have in common in order to create some common ground and establish rapport. If you know through your intelligence efforts what other projects this particular client has done, get some background on those projects and write it down. The more you know about what you are going to do and what you plan to accomplish during the meeting or presentation, the more control you will have. And it is critical that you remain in charge. If you let the client take over the meeting, you wind up doing nothing but answering his questions and defending your position.

During the presentation, do not feel that you are repeating too often. Remember the old adage: Tell them what you are going to tell them, tell them, and then tell them what you told them. Control the meeting through questions. Never make a statement when you can ask a question; get the client to make the statement in response to your question. Remember, if the client says it, he will believe it.

Keep the client involved. If necessary, have him hold things, look at things, turn the pages, help with the machinery, or whatever it takes to keep him involved. The last thing you want is a sleepy client.

Engage the client's emotions. People do not buy because of facts and figures. Instead they use facts and figures to rationalize emotional decisions. This does not mean that the facts and figures are not necessary, but do not fool yourself into thinking that they are the reasons for which clients are going to engage your services. Clients engage the services of people they feel comfortable with, and they are going to feel comfortable with people who can get them emotionally involved in their own projects. There are several emotions that come into play: greed, pride, ego, and fear are just a few examples. These are all emotions that prompt people to act. How much money can they make? How profitable is it going to be? Imagine the prestige they will have with their new project! The right decision made now can affect the future profitability of the project. The wrong decision with the wrong firm, simply for the sake of saving money in the short run, may produce disastrous effects. These are all emotional statements that should be phrased as questions to give the client a chance to state the answers, thereby reinforcing the ideas and concepts. These are the things that move your potential client to make a decision.

If you have the opportunity, and are fortunate enough, to deliver the presentation at your own office, please have the good sense to control interruptions: There should be none. This is impossible to control, however, when you meet at the client's office. The secretary pops in, a telephone call has to be returned, an important client of your potential client drops by, and so on. For one reason or another, the client is interrupted and the presentation is temporarily brought to a halt. When the client returns, you are ready to continue where you left off. Believe us when we tell you that the client is not. He must be returned to the same level of emotion and involvement he felt prior to the interruption. The way to do this is to back up just a few steps, do a brief recap of the items you have covered, obtain some minor agreements on the benefits you have previously discussed, and then continue the presentation. This small procedure following an interruption is vital if the presentation is to continue effectively.

OBJECTIONS

Most people in any line of work hate objections because they see them as roadblocks to success. One reason for this is that objections are generally misunderstood. The reason people object is because *they are interested*. The most difficult people in the world to sell are those who love everything you are doing; they cannot find one thing wrong with it and agree with everything you throw at them. But this is like trying to catch the wind—there is nothing to hang on to. Such unqualified enthusiasm is superficial, and the people showing it really have no interest whatsoever. Remember, clients make objections for two reasons:

1. They want to slow the pace down as a defense mechanism because they feel they are being pushed into a decision and want all the information necessary before making one.
2. They are asking you to help them make that decision and to give them more information. Remember, people are very fearful of making the wrong decision.

Therefore an objection might be a client's way of asking you to confirm that the decision he is going to make is the right one for him. If you view objections in this light, you will gladly handle every one that the client throws at you.

There is a difference between an objection and a condition. An objection is a defense mechanism. A condition is a real reason that prevents the client from going ahead. The potential client may not be able to get financing on a project. Believe us when we tell you that that is a condition. Or a federal law might require your firm to have something it does not have. If, for instance, you do not have liability insurance and you have no desire or inclination to get it, that is a condition, not an objection.

Because it is often difficult to tell if something is a true condition or if it is an objection, to be on the safe side treat every condition as if it were an objection. Sometimes clients are not 100 percent truthful when they say something cannot be done. These may be major objections as opposed to minor ones, but at the same time if you can break them down, they are objections, not conditions. You must therefore assume that all conditions are objections until proven otherwise.

A prime example is, "It is our company's policy not to do business with a firm that has not been in business for four years or more." That may or may not be the case. If your proposal is attractive enough and your credentials are sound, this does not have the force of law. If that company wants to do business with you, it can. If, on the other hand, you cannot break down the objection and the client holds to it, it becomes a condition.

You should learn the basic essentials for overcoming objections. If you let every objection of a client throw you, you do not stand a chance. The first thing to do when a client has an objection is to hear him out. Listen to him attentively. Then feed the objection back to him. Make him see that you understand the objection. Next, question the objection. For example, say a client tells you the following: "I'm sorry, I just don't feel comfortable using a firm that has been in business only a year and a half."

First acknowledge: "Yes, I can certainly understand that." Feed it back to him: "You say you do not feel comfortable with a firm that has been in business only a year and a half." Then question it: "Could you elaborate on that? What exactly don't you feel comfortable about?"

Many times questioning the objection provides the client with an answer: "Well, I just don't think that you have the experience we're looking for."

Restate what the client has said: "Then experience is really what you're after in an A/E firm?" The answer will be, "Well, yes, of course it is." Answer the client's objection: "Well as you can see, even though we've been in business only one and a half years, the partners that make up our firm represent over 20 years of engineering experience. Is this the kind of experience you were looking for?" Again the answer will be, "Well, yes, of course it is."

Finally confirm the answer: "Well that settles that question, doesn't it? By the way . . ." Simply confirm the answer and dispose of the objection, then go on immediately with something else.

The following are some techniques for answering objections:

1. Put them in the driver's seat. If they object to something that your company has done in the past or a service that they have not gotten for one reason or another, ask them what they would have done to solve the problem. They most likely will answer their own objection. You then simply smile and say, "That's what we did."
2. Change the emphasis of their objection. This will work quite well with minor objections. You might say, "Is it the short-term costs that are more important or the long-term profitability of the project?"
3. Use a benefit summary. If there is something minor about the proposal that they do not like, recap the things that they

do like, getting minor agreements on each point. This will deemphasize the minor objection and will help them see the overall proposal.

4. Go through a history readback. One objection that you may encounter may be, "We have used another firm for so long that we are extremely satisfied." You simply ask them if they have ever used a firm other than their current one before that. Generally the answer is yes. Are they now pleased with the change? Of course they are—they told you how pleased they were with their present company. Then basically, if they changed to get more benefits and were satisfied with the results of that decision, wouldn't they at least be interested in looking at a proposal that could also benefit them and their company as it did when they looked at the proposal of the firm they are currently with?

CLOSING

This is the final step in the selling sequence. Closing is nothing more than asking the client to agree to a decision. This is where you enter into the true negotiations. The client has agreed that you are the firm for the job and you are now ready to proceed. All other aspects of the selling sequence are absolutely useless if you cannot get past this point. Actually, the final decision is nothing but a culmination of minor decisions along the way. The basic closing technique is the assumptive close—you simply assume that you are proceeding until you are stopped. You then test the assumption with the following techniques:

The alternate of choice. Never ask a client a yes or no question. The answer will be no. Give the client alternatives: "Do you want us to put a rush on these schematics or do we have time considering the current progress of the site analysis?" Unless the client stops you, you are one step closer to entering into a contractual agreement. "Would you like this in a formal proposal or would a general outline of what we agreed on today be sufficient to begin work on the project?" Unless they stop you, you have the job.

Erroneous conclusion. Make a mistake: "Now you only want outlets around the walls, isn't that right?" If they correct you and say that they also want outlets in the center of the room near the work area, they too are assuming that you are proceeding with the project.

Answering a question with a question. The client asks you, "Is it possible to get the final design work done by the 14th?" If all you do is answer, "Yes, it is," you have nothing. Remember to answer the question with a question. "Is the 14th when you need it?" "Yes, it is." Make a note to put that into the final agreement. If they do not stop you, they are proceeding.

The similar situation close. When a client is on dead center and having a difficult time making a decision, use the similar situation close. Tell an anecdote about someone he knows and respects who was in a similar situation and what he did about it. If the client agrees that theirs probably was a good idea, make a note of that, then continue.

"I'll think it over." This is the most devastating of all objections. It means, "Go away, don't bother me. I don't want to be pressured." The problem with this objection is that there is nothing to hold on to. They are not objecting to anything. They simply want to get rid of you.

The way to handle this is to first agree with them: "Yes, any decision as important as this should be entered into with the utmost thought and care." And begin packing up to leave. Then attempt to narrow down exactly what it is that they want to think over.

Proceed with a benefit summary of the things that you have agreed to previously: "Are you concerned about the integrity that we bring with us? Is it possibly our experience? You do feel that we can bring the project in on schedule, don't you?" Proceed with several of these in relatively rapid succession. Do not give them time to say much. Then hit them with the probable final objection, one that they can agree they would like to think over: "Could it be the money?" This is one they can sink their teeth into. With such an expenditure, they really do need to think it over. Now you have a concrete objection.

Once you have established that the cost is too high, simply ask, "How much too high?" Nail them down to a figure, then take only the difference, not the entire project cost, and reduce it to the ridiculous; this is to get them to do the math. Break it out over the amortized period of 10, 20, 30 years. Then break it down to how much per day they are really talking about. Once this difference is broken down, you simply ask if the amount per day is enough to postpone a project with a potential profit of . . .? What you have done is successfully taken the "I'll think it over" and reduced it to a discussion of money that you can now handle through price negotiations using the "If we can do . . ." technique. Once they agree, your job is not to sell them on the project but to work up a proposal that meets the agreed upon cost and scope.

MOVING THE CLIENT OFF DEAD CENTER

Many times you will have made a proposal and have followed up. They are ostensibly considering it, but you cannot get them to move. This is the most frustrating of situations. You know they want to go with it, the price is right, the proposal is sound, it is in their best interest, they have no more objections, and they really like what you are doing, but they just will not move. Days go by, weeks, and nothing.

You must realize that you cannot let it simply hang. You must find out why they are not moving. In nine out of ten cases, the reason clients do not move is because they do not have the money or their financing has not been approved. And after all the negotiations, they are embarrassed. They just cannot bring themselves to tell you at this point that they cannot proceed. What has occurred is that you have eliminated all of the objections and are now down to a condition that neither of you can do anything about. You must find out if this is the reason so you do not continue to press them into further embarrassment, which could destroy the relationship that you have spent time and effort establishing. (At the same time, if this is not the reason, you do not want to simply let the matter sit. The client may become dissatisfied with you and go out looking for greener pastures.)

If financing is indeed the condition try to get an "if" close, which means that you will be ready subject to the approval of the financing. This is simply an informal agreement ostensibly so you can prepare the necessary arrangements. If for one reason or another, the financing does fall through, then no harm has been done. But when it is approved, the two of you will be ready to proceed without further delay. This gives you an excuse to follow up on minor technical points that need the client's approval, which will give you further opportunities to check on the progress of the loan application.

When following up with a potential client who is not moving, do not call up and say, "Well, have you thought it over?" The answer will always be, "Yes, we have. No." At that point you have nothing. What you must do on each follow-up is to give them something new to consider, even if it is something insignificant that you forgot to tell them the last time you were talking. Then hit them with a choice: "Oh, by the way, do you feel that we will be getting under way by the end of the month or do you think it will be about the first of next month? When approached in this manner, they will often tell you what the real objection is.

One of the absolute dead giveaways that financing is the problem is the chain of poor excuses they will come up with: one of the partners is on vacation; somebody is sick; the secretary has been absolutely swamped. These are generally things they have no control over. And they have not told you no. The poorer and poorer the excuse, the more likely that they are not dissatisfied with your proposal but that the problem is financing.

From time to time, when you do not get a positive response within a reasonable period of time from the potential client, you reevaluate the proposal and see that you could still make some money if you took the job at a lesser fee to the client. This is a very ticklish thing to handle. You cannot simply call the client up and say that you can now do the job for less money. You have to approach the client as you would for any typical follow-up and say that, after working slavishly over it, you have come up with an alternate proposal, that although it changes the scope of what you had previously proposed, your calculations show that the net effect can drastically increase the profitability of the project. You would like to have the opportunity to show them how to save some money. You have some time either Wednesday or Thursday, which would they prefer?

The crux of the matter here is that any changes whatsoever must come with a reduction of the scope of the project, no matter how minor. Under no circumstances must the client feel that by waiting he can simply make you come down on your professional fees.

WHEN NOT TO WORRY ABOUT FORMULAS

One of the things that you must understand is that formulas such as the ones in the chapter on bidding and cost estimating can drive you to the poorhouse. They must be weighed with a little common sense. For example, if on your way home from your office, as you were going to the parking lot, someone came up to you and offered you a $10 bill, would you take it? (We will assume that there is nothing dishonest or ulterior about the proposal.) Of course you would take it. The problem is that if you took the time to job cost the offer and compute it to your billing rate and included the overhead rate necessary for break-even, then considering the amount of time it took you to conduct the transaction, you would probably conclude that you lost money.

Naturally this is a ridiculous scenario. Of course you would simply take the money and run. What is wrong with the job costing? There is nothing wrong with it; your common sense simply tells you that you will make $10 if you take the money. Then what is wrong with the formulas?

Well, there is nothing wrong with the formulas either; it is just when they are applied. Let us analyze this transaction. First you were on your way home and not at work. The problem here is not that you are not at work—it is simply that you have nothing better to do with your time. Now when we say you have nothing better to do with your time we do not mean to imply that you should not go home. But the act of going home is not a profitable action. Taking the $10 is. Let us take it a step further and back to the business environment.

Assume that you have a small business employing six people: yourself, one secretary, and four A/E professionals. Let us also assume that the utilization rate of the office as a whole is 44 percent. What this means is that everyone averaged together is spending 44 percent of the available time on projects that are billable. Conversely, there is 66 percent of indirect time. If you exclude the secretary, you see that the utilization rate rises to 49 percent. In plain English, there is plenty of slack time available to do other projects.

As a result of the above analysis, you should not be surprised to see that the overhead rate for your firm is above 200 percent. This means that you are paying $2 for overhead for every $1 of direct labor. And naturally you have plugged this figure into your job costing models and are bidding out your projects accordingly. Because of this you are overbidding and losing contracts, thus lowering your utilization rate and raising your overhead rate, forcing you to bid still higher on the next project and the next project, until you are broke.

There are two forces that are at work here. First, you have slack time you are paying for. Therefore if you can channel this same labor into billable activity, you have not increased your costs at all. In fact, if you determine that, because of the low utilization rate, you can do the project with the time that is currently being channelled into indirect if you billed $5 above your hard costs for the project, you will make $5 that you would not have ordinarily made. But your formulas will tell you that you lost a bundle of money.

Does this mean that the formulas do not work? No, not at all. It simply means that you are overstaffed to let your utilization rate slip below about 60 percent. (This percentage is an arbitrary number that will need to be adjusted for break-even for each individual firm.) From a purely financial analysis, you should reduce your staff and thus raise your utilization rate and reduce your overhead if you wish to make money. If this is not a viable option for one reason or another, then you should look at projects from the angle of constant dollars made without regard to overhead until such time as the utilization rate is substantially raised.

An example of this is an A/E firm that bid out, according to the formula, a fee of $72,000. Because the overhead rate was so high, owing to a lack of work, their analysis told them that they should bid the project at this figure. The project was scheduled to last four months. Their hard costs of labor, consultants, and other direct charges were about $30,000. We will assume that $15,000 of this was for direct labor expenses, which are hard expenses to the project. They were at a 200 percent overhead rate; therefore, the formulas told them that they would make only $12,000 for this project for the four months and thus their bid.

But let us assume that the $15,000 worth of direct labor was going to be spent anyway because of the firm's inability to reduce its staff. Then there was about $30,000 worth of overhead in this bid that could have been cut out without adversely affecting the company if it got the bid. In fact in a case such as this, we would recommend that you split the difference and reduce the bid by $15,000 just to get the project. When business picks up because you are bidding lower, as the utilization rate returns to a normal position and the overhead rate becomes reasonable, you can use more exact formulas.

Let us emphasize again that this can occur immediately by a reduction of staff. And this commonsense approach should be looked at in addition to the formulas so that you will not be merely blinded by numbers and not recognize a simple rule. You cannot go broke by exchanging indirect time for direct labor dollars.

As we saw in bidding and cost estimating, depending upon the nature of your firm, the utilization rate of your employees, and where during any period or cycle you have reached break-even, the cost to you of doing a project fluctuates greatly. This technique of changing the scope of the project and reducing the fees in order to move a client off dead center is effective if there is a hook and if a close is attached with it. "If we can modify the scope of the project to where it will be acceptable to you and reduce the overall expense of the project to make it more profitable for you to proceed, would it be more in line with what you are thinking?" Try to get a commitment out of them before presenting the proposal. Remember that this must be handled delicately so it does not appear that you are having a sale on professional fees. You want to reopen the negotiations and create a win-win situation for both of you.

The sales techniques that we have discussed in this chapter are by no means the last word on selling. We have not touched on the "get 'em while they're hot" sales approaches. The purpose of this chapter was simply to highlight some of the sales techniques used in other industries and adapt them to our uses.

To some professionals techniques we have discussed may seem artificial and unprofessional. To them we say that you cannot simply mimic the words. You must practice these techniques and make them part of your own vocabulary so that when you use them, it becomes a sincere conversation between you and the client rather than simply another sales technique he can spot. If the client recognizes anything you do as a technique, it has lost its effectiveness and he will try to fight you. We do not recommend that you use everything at first. You should pick an idea that you can be comfortable with. Practice and make it your own. Use it and see the results. Then move on to another. Understand thoroughly the concepts and rationales behind the ideas. We know that the effectiveness of your presentations will increase dramatically.

Referrals

Most of the concepts that have been presented thus far were designed primarily for you to find your clients, market to those clients, sell to those clients, and negotiate and produce satisfactory contracts. As you can see, this takes a lot of work and is very time-consuming. There is one area of marketing, however, that is very easy but quite productive. It happens when a person calls you on the telephone and says, "Another client recommended that I call you. He said you do excellent work. I would like to talk to you about a project I am planning." A few of these, and you will think you are the greatest salesman on the face of the earth, but these people are presold. Based on analyses we have done for a number of clients on their sales-to-presentation ratio covering many different industries, we have found that you should sell one out of every ten potential clients that you meet. But this ratio does not apply when a client is a referred prospect. With referrals, instead of 10 percent, you should sell between 50 and 90 percent if they call you, and easily 30 percent if you call them. Many times we beat our heads against the wall, doing everything we can think of to market, when out of the blue someone picks up the telephone and says, "A client of yours referred me to you and I want your product." The question is how to create this situation more often.

The primary way to get referrals is to simply ask the clients who are pleased with you and your work to refer you. There is motivation on both sides. If your business fails, your clients have lost a good architect or engineer on whom they could count. Therefore it is in their best interest that you have quite a few customers so you prosper and remain in business. A second reason is that most of your clients, if they are pleased with you and you have a good relationship with them, honestly want to help you. Finally, there is reciprocity. Nothing comes free in this world. If they help you, you will help them in the same manner and both of you will be successful.

The next best thing to a referral who calls and asks for an appointment is to be able to use the name of the person who referred you with your own qualified clients and prospects. Naturally you will give your prospective client the names, addresses, and telephone numbers of other clients who have given you permission to use their names. The problem with this procedure is that, when you are attempting to close the sale, the potential client may not remember that he was referred to you.

What we would like to do is get a type of referral that helps to sell the client at the time we are making our presentation. One method of doing this is to have a page of quotations from your clients saying great things about you and your work. You should have about four to six quotations. These may be in your brochure or they may be on a separate sheet. Be careful to give due credit to the person (and the firm) you are quoting.

This page should be followed in your presentation by copies of several testimonial letters. These are letters from your clients, written on their letterhead, that go into great detail thanking you for the service, courteous treatment, excellent work, and so on, that they have received from you. Do not have too many in your presentation. For one thing your potential clients are not going to sit there all day long and read twenty letters of endorsement. Three or four letters should show that you have more than one happy client, yet not be too much for the potential client to read and still be impressed. You should, of course, be prepared to provide the names and addresses of other clients for more formal references as requested.

How do you go about getting referred leads, letters of endorsement, and quotations? It is really not difficult. First, provide good service so that people will have no qualms whatsoever about referring you to others. Then ask them if they would mind writing a letter that you could use when you talk with other similar clients. Most will respond that they will be more than happy to. Some are even flattered.

Do not leave it at that. Being happy to do something does not mean it will be done today. If you leave it up to them, you might have to nag them for a letter, and that is the last thing you want to do to good clients. Many of the people you will be dealing with are very busy individuals who do not have time to sit down and dictate a letter. Offer to draft one out, bring it over, and have them read (and edit) it; then simply have their secretary type it, and get it signed. This is also in your best interest because left to their own devices, your clients will all write similar letters.

By helping them in this manner, you can stress any particular aspect of your product or service that is appropriate. The reason for the diversity of letters is not only to show the number of clients that you have, but also to be able to point out certain things to potential clients without having to say them yourself—they can read what others have said about your firm.

If you have not received a letter in a week, try for a quotation. Call your clients back and reiterate that you know how busy they have been. Mention that the last time you talked, they made a good point about some aspect of your services and ask if they would mind if you mentioned that to other clients.

The main referral that you are after is the referred lead. There are basically three things that you would like your clients to do in order to refer you.

First, you would like your client to call potential clients and tell them that what they really need to do is to talk to you. If you can create this kind of enthusiasm on the part of your clients, most of them will be more than happy to spread the good news of what they have found. In addition, if you have provided good service and a quality product at a reasonable cost, it shows how good they are to have found you initially. Once you get a client to do this for you, wait about a week. This is to give the potential client a chance to call you before you call him. There is a distinct psychological advantage to having these people call you rather than your calling them. But do not let the lead go cold waiting for them to call you. Telephone the potential client and say that your client has asked you to call; then attempt to make the appointment.

The second thing your client can do for you is to let you use his name. If this is all he is willing to do for you, take it. Then pick up the phone and use his name as an introduction when contacting the prospect.

The third thing you would like when a client agrees to refer you is permission for you to invite a potential client to call him for a reference.

It is important that you get as many of these commitments as possible up front. The best time to ask for referrals is in the early stages of a project, while the enthusiasm is still new. This also has a secondary benefit. If a client has already committed to giving you a recommendation, he has a vested interest in making this relationship work, and this enhances your ability to work with the client.

Finally one of the keys to working with referrals is to make sure that you never lose contact, even with previous customers. Previous customers can be of great assistance to you even if they do not have a current project or a need for your service. Never let them die on the vine; keep in constant contact. Drop by to see them, send them letters, remember their birthdays, send thank-you notes, and so on. You must remain constantly on their minds in order to continue receiving referrals from them. In turn, you must call the client periodically and give that client leads or information that will be useful to him. Referrals are a two-way street. We guarantee you that if you work to help your clients grow and prosper, they will do the same for you.

Conclusion

It is important to remember that as a professional you have an obligation to your profession. You should also remember that you are now in business for yourself and that you have an obligation to that business. In a capitalistic society, all businesses are forced by their very nature to compete, and there are no exceptions. One of the questions you must ask yourself is, Am I willing to compete? Competition is nothing more than offering better service or a better product at a lower price. This is the same thing that you ask of the people you do business with when you are the purchaser. You should give nothing less to those clients who use your A/E services. Competition is not a dirty word. Going head-to-head with someone else who wishes to sell the same thing to the same client is truly the "American way."

What we have attempted to do here is to put down in an organized manner the course of action that you can take to increase the number of clients you have and improve the manner in which you sell and service those clients. It is not easy. The selling of architectural and engineering services is really in many ways no different from selling anything else. Therein lies the key.

You may agree or disagree with many things in this part, but none of them is going to do you any good until you begin to apply them. Even if you simply use one technique—the mailing list, the telephone calls, or possibly the sales techniques, for example—when you are in front of your client, you will drastically increase the profitability of your firm. Remember, one of the most important things about marketing is that the marketing techniques must become a natural part of you. If clients perceive your actions to be a technique or some kind of trick to get them to do something, they will be resistant. Therefore what you choose to do must become a part of you. This applies not only to selling, but also to the routine things that the client never sees, such as how you set up your data base, how you go about making your telephone calls, and so on. If you do not feel comfortable doing these things, they are not yet yours. The only way to feel comfortable doing something new is to do it a little at a time, until you are so sure of yourself that it becomes natural for you.

You may be saying to yourself, "How can I do every last thing in this book, apply every last technique, do all the mailing lists, make all the telephone calls, send out all the news releases, do all the investigative work on my clients and competitors, and still find enough hours in the day to do my other work?" You may want to ask yourself whether you should consider hiring a full-time person to handle all this. Look at your average fees. For many A/E firms, these can be anywhere from $20,000 to $50,000 profit on a project that lasts three to six months. In fact many firms cannot survive on the number of projects they get unless the fees are high enough to keep their employees working. Even a small architectural or engineering firm may have fees of $8,000 to $10,000 or even $15,000 per project. You must ask yourself this: If you hired an individual to implement the techniques presented here and paid this individual $25,000 to $30,000 per year or more, how many projects would this individual have to secure for your firm at your average fees and still break-even? Only you can answer the question of whether an individual of this type can be cost-effective for your firm.

The fact of the matter is that somebody has to do it. Your marketing must be more than shaking hands with people at the local Rotary Club meeting or making a simple announcement in the Chamber of Commerce newsletter. Marketing is a full-time job. The question is, Who is going to do it? Naturally the person best suited for it should be the one to do it. This may be the owner, or the project manager, or an individual who is hired specifically for this duty. Those firms that ignore marketing, even in the good times, are the firms that will not be around in the bad times.

Please do yourself a favor and at least begin. Start an organized marketing campaign and continue it for at least six months. Remember that many times you will not see the results of your marketing for three to six months, but if you apply even a few of the ideas and techniques found here you will be successful.

PART 3
COST MANAGEMENT

Introduction

Everyone knows the proverb "A penny saved is a penny earned." The author obviously did not live in twentieth-century America and face the bite of the Internal Revenue Service. Actually, much depends on what type of penny got earned and what type got saved. Because the difference can sometimes mean two pennies earned for the penny saved.

It is a fact of life today that it takes money to make money (pardon another tired cliché). And we are not simply talking about investments. Rarely is there a business that does not calculate its variable costs and expenses for every dollar of revenue. This is because there are certain expenses that must be met in order to create business and, in turn, revenue.

This brings us to the purpose of this part of the book. What we want to make you aware of is that all costs were not created equal. Almost all firms waste enormous amounts of money. Actually, the more profitable a firm is, the more money it can afford to waste. We want to emphasize that you can increase profits by cutting costs just as well as by increasing revenue.

Obviously there is more than one type of cost, so the first thing you must do is to identify all of your expenses and classify these in categories. Once you know what kinds of costs you are looking at, it should be much easier to properly evaluate them and their effects on the company and its profitability.

We will give you several techniques for cost cutting and for properly evaluating whether to make an expenditure or not. Once you have properly classified your costs, you will see how certain types of expenditures bring with them other hidden expenditures that were not evident at first and how it is possible to shift certain types of costs from one classification to another in order to save money.

One of the really important issues we will be working with concerns budgeting. Most people do not know how to budget or how to use the budget as a tool to help control costs without straitjacketing the company. Good cost management can help minimize many of the pitfalls and maximize profits for your firm.

Many of the topics covered in this part of the book may, on

the surface, seem obvious to you. Even if you are aware of all of the techniques found here, being aware and using them are two entirely different things. There will also be some ideas and techniques that are not necessarily applicable to your company. This may be because of the size of your firm or because you have not experienced a certain problem yet. What we want you to do is to use this book cafeteria-style, picking and choosing the things that you need.

The Cost Analysis Survey

In this chapter you will find the Cost Analysis Survey (see page 172), an extremely useful tool for evaluating the need and cost benefit ratio of a projected expenditure. It should also be used during the decision-making process of any major prospective purchase. You should use a separate sheet for each prospective purchase and for each expenditure that you are comparing. Therefore feel free to make as many copies as necessary of this form.

The Cost Analysis Survey is simply an analytical tool that asks certain questions concerning your proposed or existing expenditures. You provide the answers by assigning a number from 1 to 5 (1 being not applicable and 5, extremely applicable) to determine the degree of agreement you have with the statements as they relate to the proposed expenditure. At the end you simply add up the numbers. This is to give you a mathematical value for the expenditure. For example, one with a value of 70 is probably a better expenditure than one with a 35. Keep in mind, however, that these figures are *subjective* and therefore there are no "passing" grades for anything.

The reason absolutes are not possible with instruments such as this is that on the same expenditure one firm will assign a value of 4 and another a 2. As a result one company may find that a good expenditure is one that results in a score of 62, while another may be happy with expenditures at a level of 47. Both companies can be using the instrument properly and it will be performing its task equally well.

IS THE EXPENSE CRITICAL?

The word *critical* means different things to different individuals. There are, of course, some expenditures—taxes, for example—that everyone agrees are critical. If you do not pay the IRS, they will close down your business and/or put you in jail. Other expenditures are more subjective. If you definitely feel that an expense is critical to the firm it does not matter what the score on the Cost Analysis Survey is: The funds must be expended

Figure 5

Cost Analysis Survey

_______ 1. The expense replaces other existing costs equal to or greater than the proposed expense.

_______ 2. The expense produces income equal to or greater than the expense it replaces.

_______ 3. The expense increases the quality of work.

_______ 4. The expense is based on *true* need rather than impulse.

_______ 5. The ratio of cost to quality-benefit is advantageous in comparison to other alternatives.

_______ 6. Indicate the degree to which the expense *totally* fulfills the need.

_______ 7. Indicate the degree to which the expense *cannot* be postponed.

_______ 8. Is the expense in a (1) deflationary or (5) inflationary cycle?

_______ 9. Can you match the expense (periodically) with a corresponding periodic income?

_______ 10. Does the expense fall within predetermined budgetary considerations?

_______ 11. Indicate the degree to which the expense can be used as an effective marketing tool.

_______ 12. Are there (1) tax costs or (5) tax benefits to the expense?

_______ 13. Is there a cost overhead—People?

_______ 14. Is there a cost overhead—Materials?

_______ 15. Is there (1) a better opportunity for the use of the money or is this (5) the best opportunity?

_______ Total

and, therefore, there is no need to proceed with the form. There are, however, some types of expenditures that you might think are critical but may not be at their current or proposed level. Note that this instrument should be used only on discretionary expenditures. This is where firms tend to get into trouble.

You might consider the rent payments on your place of business a critical expense, and in many ways it is. If you do not pay your rent, you could be out on the street and out of business. But is it critical at the level that you are paying? That is the question. There are many critical expenditures that are necessary but may be secured at a lower price. We are not suggesting that you discount such factors as comfort or prestige. What we want you to do is use this instrument to look objectively at your expenditures and see exactly what you are paying for. Your answer might help you avoid rationalizing a desire into a need. So although rent is indeed a critical expenditure, you might want to use the survey to compare levels of expenditures, or if you are contemplating a move, to compare rental options.

Another example is cost of goods sold. The term is used here to indicate the direct salary expenses of your employees. You are "selling" services, and your profit is on your direct labor. This is not to belittle the professional service, expertise, and ability you have to offer your clients. But the fact of the matter is that you hire people to do projects for you, and you charge a fee based on your cost of materials and labor. If you do not pay for your materials and labor, you cannot "sell" them and thus cannot bring in as much income. Therefore these costs are critical. Although you do have some discretion as to the quality of the products you sell and the quality and efficiency of the professionals you hire, once the employee is hired and the goods decided on, the expenditures cease to be discretionary and become critical.

Many times after you have finished the survey, you will find that an expenditure has become very necessary to your company and, as the analysis shows, is now critical to you because of the amount of money it can make or save your firm. This is what the survey is designed to do. You will notice from the questions that it is heavily weighted in favor of those expenditures that can save you money or make money for you. The survey is an attempt to put down in black and white the degree of importance an expenditure has in terms of profitability to your firm. In this way you can add some objectivity to your decision-making process. It can help you feel comfortable in proceeding with good decisions and in understanding and backing away from bad decisions. We have seen too many people let their emotions carry them to either extreme. More often than not, they will simply make no decision out of fear of making a mistake. Often the decision not to buy can be a worse mistake than buying the wrong thing.

Therefore, ask yourself, Is the expense critical? If you answer yes, then you should not proceed with the evaluation of the expense unless you are interested in evaluating the level of the expenditure. If you answer no, go on with the rest of the evaluation.

DEGREE OF AGREEMENT

The next step is to indicate with a number from 1 to 5 the degree of agreement you have with the statements that follow and place the number in the blank beside each on the form. Keep in mind that a 1 indicates virtually no agreement (or not applicable) and a 5 indicates total agreement (or extremely applicable). The numbers 2, 3, and 4 are for the degrees in between.

1. The expense replaces other existing costs equal to or greater than the proposed expense.

If the expense is not going to replace an existing expense, or if the new expense's savings are not equal to or greater than the replaced expense, you should enter a 1. Anything above a 1 should be the degree to which the new expense saves you money.

2. The expense produces income equal to or greater than the expense it replaces.

If the expense is not designed to produce income, you should code it a 1. If it is anticipated that the expense will produce income equal to the expense it is replacing, code it a 2. If the new expense produces income in excess of the expense it is replacing, code it 3, 4, or 5 relative to the additional income it will bring in.

3. The expense increases the quality of work.

If the expense does not affect the quality of work that is performed, code it a 1. Use 2, 3, 4, and 5 relative to the increase in the quality of work.

4. The expense is based on true *need rather than impulse.*

This question requires you to determine the need on a graded scale of 1 to 5. The greater the need for the item or expense, the higher the number should be coded.

5. The ratio of cost to quality-benefit is advantageous in comparison to other alternatives.

This question asks you to compare the proposed expense with other alternatives. The other alternatives may be competing proposals or may actually be two different ways to do the same thing. The question is asking you to evaluate the differences in quality and additional benefits between alternatives as compared to the cost. Desire, pride of ownership, or other emotional considerations may all be important in the purchase, but should not be considered in this question. It is designed simply to determine if there is a reason of quality and benefit to justify the cost.

6. Indicate the degree to which the expense totally *fulfills the need.*

Many times when we are proposing a purchase we have a wish list of things that we would like the item to do for us. We have needs. Without needs we probably should not be making the investment. Unfortunately, not many things totally fulfill those needs. Many times there is a trade-off. Other times it is a matter of economics. This question simply asks you to evaluate the proposed expense in terms of what your total needs for the item are.

7. Indicate the degree to which the expense cannot *be postponed.*

Code this item a 1 if the expense can be postponed indefinitely. Code it 2, 3, or 4, depending on the urgency of the expense and a 5 if it must be expended now.

8. Is the expense in a (1) deflationary or (5) inflationary cycle?

If the product you anticipate purchasing is in a deflationary cycle, prices tend to drop the longer you wait to purchase the item, and so it should be coded a 1. If prices are going up, it should be coded a 5. For degrees in between use 2, 3, or 4.

9. Can you match the expense (periodically) with a corresponding periodic income?

Many expenses are easily matched with a corresponding income. For example the purchase of a CAD system or other income-producing items will tend to produce income at the same rate as the expenditure for the purchase of the item. If expenditure matches income closely, it receives a 5. If you cannot match the payout with the income, it receives a 1.

10. Does the expense fall within predetermined budgetary considerations?

This is a fancy way of saying, Can I afford it? As you will learn later in the book, a budget is a guideline to help you match corresponding income with expenditures so at the end of your fiscal year you have more income than expenditures. It is not a straitjacket, but at the same time it should not be ignored. If this expenditure is totally outside of the budget, it should be coded 1. If it is planned for, it should be coded 5. The middle numbers 2, 3, and 4 represent the degree to which you can fit it into the budget dollar amounts, even at the expense, possibly, of another expenditure.

11. Indicate the degree to which the expense can be used as an effective marketing tool.

There are many expenditures that do nothing, nor do they in and of themselves increase revenue. But they are used as marketing tools to bring in new clients and as a result help to bring in additional revenue. A CAD system may be considered in this light. For many A/E firms it presents a competitive edge above and beyond its productivity advantage. As more and more A/E firms get these systems, however, the CAD will lose its marketing advantage and simply be a requirement for operation, as a drafting board is today. The more the expense can be used for marketing, the higher the coding.

12. Are there (1) tax costs or (5) tax benefits to the expense?

As you are beginning to see, not all expenses are created equal. Some expenses cost you money in taxes and other expenses are tax neutral. A tax savings should be coded 5 and a tax loss, 1. If the expense is tax neutral (besides being deductible as a whole), it should be coded 3.

13. Is there a cost overhead—People?

There are many expenditures that carry with them other hidden costs. A large computer system would be an example. The larger the computer system, the more likely you are to need a specialized individual to operate the system. The higher the cost overhead is, the lower the coding; the lower the cost overhead, the higher the coding.

14. Is there a cost overhead—Materials?

Use the same criteria as in item 13, but in relation to materials and supplies.

15. Is there (1) a better opportunity for the use of the money or is this (5) the best opportunity?

Simply stated, can you use your scarce resources (money) to better advantage? There may be absolutely nothing wrong with your proposed expenditure. For example, you may decide to market through print media. This may be perfectly acceptable. But will it bring in better results than a direct mail campaign of an equal dollar amount? If this is the best opportunity for the use of the money, it should be coded 5.

There is nothing absolute about the numbers generated by this survey. It is simply an attempt to analyze quantitatively each expenditure so that it can be compared with other expenditures.

Therefore when used properly it can be a useful tool. You may wish to experiment with the survey by adding items you feel are important to your company and possibly deleting items that are not of value to you. There are no ironclad rules. The survey is simply a tool you can use to take a good hard look at where your money is going.

Types of Costs

Not all costs and expenditures are the same. For this reason they are often grouped into different categories so that they can be handled in groups and totaled up as such to show in large areas how money is being spent. In accounting terms this is called a *chart of accounts*. Let us take a look at several types of categories for expenses and how they should be used and viewed.

VARIABLE—FIXED

This is one of the most common large divisions of expenditures used by accountants for a wide variety of firms. It defines all expenditures as being either variable or fixed.

Fixed Expenditures

A fixed expenditure is simply one that is required to open the doors of your business every day, whether or not you sell anything, have any clients, have any projects, or make any money. Fixed expenditures are not necessarily fixed as to amount of money, although their variations from month to month or period to period will of course be less drastic than the variable expenditures.

Fixed expenses are generally thought of as overhead. They include such things as rent, insurance, certain salaries (which we will discuss later), utilities (maybe), leases, supplies (maybe), and so on. As you can see, many of these categories overlap. What is important is that these expenses are recurring. They are nondiscretionary and required as an operation of business whether you have any business or not. They are in no way dependent on the sales you make or other variable criteria.

Fixed expenses are useful in determining your company's break-even point. If your fixed expenses total $1000 per month, the first $1000 profit each month must be used to pay these before you make any money. It is at this point that break-even occurs. We will talk more about break-even analysis and its effect later.

Variable Expenditures

In addition to changing from period to period, variable expenses are dependent on certain outside criteria. In most firms one such criterion is sales. For the most part, the more you sell the higher your variable expenses. Sometimes, but not always, the converse is true: The higher your variable expenses, the higher your sales.

The most important and easily recognizable variable expense is cost of goods sold. This is simply the wholesale cost of any item you sell. Naturally, the more you sell the higher your cost of goods. As you can imagine, you would not want to hold your cost of goods sold to a budget and say, "I'm sorry. We have reached our budget limit and cannot sell any more." That would be ludicrous.

Other very common variable expenses might be sales tax expense, reimbursable items, direct project supplies, or consultant expenses.

Some not so easily recognizable expenses are salaries, utilities, storage costs, and postage. Each of these are dependent on the type of business you are engaged in. If your architectural firm does space planning and sells furniture, then you have a cost of goods sold. You might also have a storage problem where the expense may vary in direct relationship to the amount of furniture you are selling during any given period of time.

Marketing expenses would definitely be variable since they are tied, you hope, directly to the amount of business they are capable of creating.

Salaries depend on the type of operation you are running. If every person in your organization is guaranteed either a certain salary or a certain number of hours, then salaries are fixed expenses even though they may vary depending on the amount of overtime required to complete projects.

What is important in this case is that you are obligated to meet your payroll whether your employees have 100 percent direct time or have not worked on a single project.

There are, however, certain salaries that are truly variable. These may fall under the category of temporary, contract labor, and the like. Contractors routinely hire employees only when they have work. If it rains, the employee may be guaranteed a couple of hours but generally is sent home. Therefore the labor expense is directly tied into the income-related projects. In this sense it is indeed variable because the labor expenses will increase directly in relationship with the income.

The important factor about variable expenses is that they represent a percentage of income. It is important that this percentage be constantly monitored. The percentage of variable expenses to revenue is an important ratio used in determining break-even. It can also become an important indicator as to the financial health of the company.

Variable-Direct Break-even Analysis

The basic formula for variable-direct break-even is:

$$VR \times I - FE = 0.$$

VR is the variable expense to income ratio expressed as the percentage profit. For example if the variable expenses are 30 percent of income, the *VR* should be .7 since 70 percent of income is available to offset the fixed expenses. *I* is income and *FE* is fixed expenses. Therefore if we want to know how much income will be necessary for break-even (or if we want to check the result of the above equation by solving for *I*) then:

$$I = FE/VR.$$

If fixed expenses are $4000.00 per month and variable expenses are 40 percent of income ($VR = .6$) $6,666.66 of income would be needed to reach break-even:

$$I = 4000/.6.$$

Direct Expenses

Another way of looking at a major division of expenses is to divide them into indirect and direct. Basically a direct expense is any expense that is required for a billable project. This is quite a useful division for any firm that is basically a time-based business rather than a product-based one.

Many people try to equate direct and indirect equally with

variable and fixed. Although there are some parallels, these classifications are definitely not the same. It is true that most fixed expenses are indirect and most direct expenses are variable, but this is not always the case.

An example of this is salaries. With the fixed-variable classification, all payroll is fixed even though a substantial amount of time may be directly related to billable projects. This is because the employees must be paid regardless of what they are doing at work. With direct-indirect, the salary of each individual employee would be divided into indirect salary and direct salary, based on exactly the amount of work that is directly related to projects.

Indirect Expenses

If direct expenses are all those expenses that are directly related to the completion of a billable project, indirect expenses are all other expenses.

Just as fixed expenses are generally referred to as overhead in the fixed-variable division, indirect expenses are also referred to as overhead.

This is where one of the biggest problems for A/E firms occurs. Obviously the term *overhead* is in question. If, as we have seen, fixed expenses and indirect expenses are not the same, there cannot be two definitions of overhead. And if overhead is different, how should you compute break-even?

Direct-Indirect Break-even Analysis

Basically the formula for direct-indirect break-even analysis is the same as for fixed-variable. The difference is mainly in the fact that indirect expenses tend to fluctuate much more. Variable expenses are for the most part stable as a percentage of income. Also those firms using the variable-fixed division generally have a product rather than time and there is a definite cost of goods sold.

With an A/E firm, there is generally no product per se; rather what it sells is time. Therefore a more meaningful percentage than the ratio of variable expenses to income is the overhead rate.

The overhead rate is a ratio of direct salaries to indirect expenses. The formula for this ratio is: indirect expenses: direct salaries.

Because this ratio can fluctuate wildly from month to month, it is important to use a 12-month moving average. The ratios are added for 12 months then divided by 12. When a month is added, the earliest month is dropped.

Before you can come up with a break-even formula for the company, even with a constant overhead rate, you must first start with an assumption that you are making a profit on the direct salary which is, for this purpose, your goods sold. Let us say that your overhead rate is 150 percent. This means that for every $1.00 of direct salary you spend you must charge $1.50 more to cover the indirect expenses or the overhead. If you are doing this you must bill out 2.5 times your cost of direct labor ($1.00 + $1.50) to break-even on each hour billed. Notice that this is *before profit.*

Therefore the indirect break-even formula is:

$$I = (Ind/OR)\,(OR + 1).$$

I is income, Ind is indirect expenses, and OR is overhead rate. Therefore if your monthly indirect expenses are $4000.00 and your overhead rate is 150 percent, you will need $6,666.66 in revenue to reach break-even:

$$(4000/1.50)\,(2.50) = 6{,}666.66.$$

Remember this is break-even and does not include profit. To check the result of the indirect break-even formula, you can solve for zero:

$$I - (Ind/OR)\,(OR + 1) = 0.$$

The two methods of dividing expenses discussed above are used as the main divisions for a general ledger chart of accounts. We recommend that merchandizing firms use variable-fixed and that A/E and other time-based firms use direct-indirect.

When using the direct-indirect division for your general ledger, first create these two categories. To make analysis easier, subtotal the direct expenses separately from the indirect. Some accountants prefer to also subtract the direct charges from the fee revenue to get a net revenue similar to a net of cost of goods sold.

TAXABLE COSTS

There are certain costs that by their expenditure create a tax obligation. The most ominous of these is the payroll expense. The tax obligation created by every dollar of payroll expenditure is a major one for any firm. Let us look at just a few of these taxes.

Matching FICA

We are all familiar with this one. It is the amount of Social Security tax that must be deposited in the Social Security fund for every dollar of payroll expenditure. It is called matching because it roughly parallels the contribution made by the employee. These taxes have a limit based on a maximum annual salary of the employee.

Unemployment Insurance

There are two of these. First there is the unemployment insurance tax you must pay to your state to support the state unemployment insurance program. The second is a federal unemployment tax (FUTA), which is used for the same purpose but on a federal level. Both of these taxes are based on a percentage of the payroll to a given limit.

General Liability Insurance

Although this is not a tax per se, it acts as a tax in a hidden way. Most general liability insurance policy premiums are based on gross payroll by given classifications. This generally means that the higher your payroll is, the higher your premiums will be for the same amount of coverage.

Workmen's Compensation Insurance

The workmen's compensation insurance laws differ from state to state. But basically this insurance is required in most states and is based directly on the actual payroll expended. Different classifications of employees have different rates. Therefore the higher the payroll of high-risk classified employees, the higher the premium.

Other Taxes

There are several other minor types of taxes on expenditures and these vary from state to state. Sales tax is one of these, but some are more obscure. One that we ran across was a tax paid by the insured for the privilege of spending money with an insurance company not licensed by the state. The theory was that if the insurance company was not going to pay the tax, the consumer would have to pay it.

INVESTMENT COSTS

An investment cost is one that brings a return which equals or exceeds the initial investment. For example, certain seminar costs might be classified as investment costs because the benefits gained would result in additional income for the company.

More direct investment costs might be in capital expenditures. These are usually made with the anticipation that the additional equipment will bring about more productivity and thus produce more income. A/E automation is a prime example of this type of cost.

Marketing costs are also considered to be investment costs. The old axiom that it takes money to make money was never truer. Some investment costs are readily identifiable with the direct return on the investment. The money spent on marketing often is not as direct. But you must have a systematic plan for the expenditure of this money and it should be spent consistently in order to begin to receive a return on the investment in terms of more revenue.

HIDDEN COSTS

A hidden cost is an unanticipated cost that is a result of another expenditure. As noted above, additional premiums on insurance caused by the expenditure of payroll expenses is a hidden cost.

Other types of hidden costs might be additional expenditures required by the initial expenditure. An example of this is a large computer system that requires additional personnel to operate the machinery. This in turn may create other costs, and so on.

The classification of expenditures has several practical applications. The division of variable-fixed and direct-indirect has applications to overhead rate, break-even analysis and other formulas.

By identifying the type of expenditure, you should be able to evaluate hidden costs and possibly to shift expenditures from payroll to other types of expenditures.

Funny Money

It has been said that you can prove anything with statistics. Well you can do even worse with accounting. You can create money that does not exist. There is nothing magical about this. Bankers have been doing it since the sixteenth century. We strongly recommend, however, that your accountant guide you in the way your books are kept for the IRS and for management and banking purposes.

It is incumbent on you to learn just enough about accounting to understand how this is done. There is nothing extremely difficult about the principles of accounting and we will take just a few paragraphs to explain it.

There are basically three types of accounts: asset, liability, and capital. The term *capital* tends to confuse many people. It is simply your net ownership or net worth of the company.

The basic formula in accounting is assets = liability + capital. Since assets represent things that you own (including cash) and liabilities represent people you owe, the accounting formula is better stated as capital = assets − liabilities. Your net worth is equal to what you *own* less what you *owe*.

Now in order to keep straight what you owe and what you own, accountants have developed what they call a double entry accounting system. For example, if you borrow money and put it in your checking account, you increase two accounts, not just one. Your checking (assets) account increases by the amount of money you deposit and the loan (liability) account increases by the amount of money you borrow. Therefore two entries are made that increase cash (an asset) and the loan (a liability). Therefore, since equal amounts were added to both sides, your capital or net worth has not changed.

In addition to the three types of accounts mentioned above, there are two more: revenue and expense. Generally speaking, revenue is what you bring in (income), and expenses are what it cost you to make that revenue. Bear in mind that there is a whole array of legal definitions and IRS interpretations as to what comprises revenue and expenses. For our purposes, however, revenue and expenses are simply side accounts that are added together and the net added to capital. These two accounts are called contra accounts to capital.

In summary, the more income *(revenue)* over expenditures *(expenses)* you have, the more money you make and therefore you increase your *assets*. Thus as assets increase without an increase in *liabilities*, your net worth *(capital)* increases.

The only thing complicated about accounting is keeping score. Debit and credit are synonymous with add and subtract, but both debits and credits each add and subtract, depending on the type of account. Just remember that there is no real value to a debit or credit in and of itself. It simply depends on the type of account it affects.

All you need to do to keep debits and credits straight is to know whether an account is a *debit account* or a *credit account*. The following are the account types:

Assets: Debit Account	Debit *debit accounts* to add
Liabilities: Credit Account	Credit *debit accounts* to subtract
Capital: Credit Account	Credit *credit accounts* to add
Revenue: Credit Account	Debit *credit accounts* to subtract
Expenses: Debit Account	

Remember: You debit *debit accounts* to add to them, and credit *debit accounts* to subtract from them; you credit *credit accounts* to add to them, and debit *credit accounts* to subtract from them.

Therefore when you receive cash revenue you must debit cash (asset account) to increase cash and credit revenue to increase revenue. Remember that for every entry you must have equal dollar amounts of debits and credits. This is what is meant by debits and credits being in balance.

Needless to say this is not meant to make an accountant out of anyone. The purpose here is to give some background to those of you who do not understand accounting so that we can demonstrate how the accounts can be manipulated.

The only thing that is required in accounting is that the debits equal the credits at all times. Therefore every time we spend money we are not required to call it an expense. We call it an expense only if we debit an expense account. But what if we were to debit an asset account instead. What effect would that have on our net worth or income statement?

A legitimate example of this would be an insurance policy that you prepay for the upcoming year. The reason we say that you are prepaying it is that you pay the annual premium in one month, but this is for all 12 upcoming months. The proper way to do this is to credit (reduce) cash and debit (increase) an asset account called prepaid insurance. As each month progresses, you debit (increase) the expense of insurance and credit (reduce) the asset prepaid insurance. Your net result in the initial payment of the insurance policy was simply to swap one asset for another one. You swapped cash for an asset called prepaid insurance. You did not spend any money. Therefore even though you have less cash the company is theoretically in the same financial position.

There is no effort in accounting to judge the relative quality of an asset. In most people's minds, cash is the most important asset and really the only one that counts. In fact an accounting teacher once said that the only thing he ever trusted on a balance sheet was the cash because he could count it. Although this is an exaggeration, he may not be far off. Of course, if all of your assets were cash, you could not be in business.

Let us look at how the various accounts can be manipulated. Most firms are, or should be, on what is called an accrual accounting system at least for management purposes. On this type of system, expenses are accounted for when they are incurred, not when they are paid. And revenue is recognized when projects are billed out, not when clients get around to paying.

This kind of management information is useful when you try to match revenue with its corresponding expenditure—the only way you know if you are making any money. The way this is done is very simple. When you send out your bills, you debit trade receivables (an asset account) and credit revenue for the new money on the bills. When the invoices are paid, you debit cash (assets) because the money came in and credit trade receivables to reduce the receivables owed.

Remember, this type of accounting is not only perfectly proper, it is generally preferred. But notice the effect. The value of the company increased by the amount of the revenue entry. In essence what you did was to create value with a paper entry. To show you the power of this entry, a banker will loan you money on it.

Since you can so easily create money by a paper entry, must

be careful that the receivables your customers owe are good. If they are not, you are accounting for money you do not have and will never get.

Another method of creating money on paper is through capital investment. What this means is that you purchase something large, such as a piece of equipment. IRS regulations generally require you to capitalize these expenditures—to delay the expense until a future time. Each year, for a predetermined number of years, you expend a portion of the investment. This future expenditure is called depreciation. How this is done is set forth by IRS codes. What is of interest here is the effect depreciation has on your profits.

If you buy a CAD system for $10,000 cash, then cash leaves your bank account, but you have simply swapped one asset, $10,000 cash, for equipment of equal value. Therefore no change has occurred in your balance sheet. Each year you get to depreciate a portion of this equipment. Therefore in future years, your income is reduced by this depreciation expense. The interesting thing about depreciation is that it does not affect cash. Therefore in future years, depreciation increases your expenses without a corresponding reduction in cash. There is a reduction in the asset, but it is in the value of the equipment.

A marginally acceptable technique is to create a deferred asset. This is used when you have had a bad month and the last thing you want to do is to compound it with an out of the ordinary expenditure. Rather than treat it as an expense, which it may well be this month, defer the expenditure by creating an asset called deferred assets. The entry would be a credit to cash and debit to the deferred asset. Naturally this will eventually have to be closed out as a credit to the deferred asset and a debit to the expenditure. But through this method the expenditure can be deferred and not counted against the income statement.

One of the more interesting practices among A/E firms is an account called unearned or unbilled income. It might go by other names, but it is an attempt to account for income before it is billed. This has some validity for those firms that do not bill out a phase until it is 100 percent complete. If they did not use this practice they would be understating their income until billing and then overstating the income for the month in which it was billed out. In using this method, simply add up the amount expended in direct labor and apply a billing charge for any that is not reflected on the invoices. Then simply treat it as a "receivable." When the invoice is actually sent, the unbilled amount is reversed and the receivable is established.

It is our purpose to point out that not all money is created equal. It is very common for a rapidly growing company to be making a mint and still run out of money. They are generating rampant receivables through sales at the same time they are investing in equipment for expansion. The problem is they are using cash for the investment in the equipment and are not receiving equal and timely cash payments on their receivables. This is where a good banker can come in handy.

One of the hardest things to convince people of is that a loan repayment is not an expense. Only the interest on the loan is an expense. When the loan is made, a debit is made to cash and a credit to notes payable. As the loan is repaid, cash is credited and the loan debited for the principal amount only. Anything above the principal amount is debited to the interest expense account. The confusion comes in the income and expenses and cash flow (cash flow will be discussed in detail in the next chapter).

The most commonly asked question concerning accounting is, "We made a profit. Where's the money?" The purpose of this chapter has been to try to answer that question. Your accountant can prepare a very valuable report called an analysis of changes in financial condition (otherwise referred to as the where got, where gone statement). This involves taking the income statement for any period of time, subtracting out expenses that do not affect cash, such as depreciation, and adding in cash expenditures that are not on the income statement. In this way you can balance cash flow with the income statement.

When you look at an income statement, remember that there is generally no relationship between cash and income. As you can see from the discussion above, there are many variables that can affect cash. Keep in mind that cash is simply one more asset account, albeit a very important one.

Cash Management

Cash is simply just another asset account. It is, of course, a vital asset account. When you run out of cash, you lose. Therefore the proper management of cash is vital to any company.

As we saw in the last chapter, there is no relationship between an income statement and cash flow. Both are important, however, and should not be ignored.

LOANS

A client recently told us that he did not believe in borrowing money on his receivables. This is an admirable goal, but many times a growing company cannot afford that luxury, especially if there is a downturn in the economy and many well-paying clients simply slow down the payment of their bills. If this happens, the company can continue to grow and be profitable but at the same time face a cash emergency.

It is therefore prudent for every firm to set up a line of credit with a bank for at least 50 percent of outstanding receivables at any point in time. A/E firms are notorious for having high receivables. If you have been in business for any period of time, we do not have to convince you of the wisdom of having a good banker who can supply you with ready cash.

The important thing is not the ability to borrow money, but to borrow it wisely. The mistake that most firms make is that they do not properly classify and manage the different types of loans that are available. A line of credit loan should be used simply to act as a stand-in for outstanding receivables so that they can be treated and used the same as cash. What this means is that as the receivables are paid in, the line of credit needs to be paid down.

Many times this is not possible. You may want to purchase additional equipment. But this type of loan is not for that purpose. The line of credit loan is a short-term loan. You should go back to your banker and get an expansion loan, which is longer-term.

The other abuse that is difficult to control is the use of the credit line for operation without an increase in the receivables. Sometimes there is no other way if the company is losing money. And if you have to, you have to. Accrual accounting is the only way to let you know if your use of the line of credit is legitimate or if you are flirting with disaster. Of course it lets your banker know as well.

Remember that there is a cost to receivables. This is called interest and is the way bankers make money. The interest charged on loans is substantially higher than the interest the bank pays on your accounts. This means it is better to pay down on your line of credit than to keep the money in a savings or money market account.

This is not true for an expansion loan. Unless your cash position is substantially high or unless you can add the amount you pay off the expansion loan to the line of credit, you should not use current cash for early payments of these types of loans. The reason is that unless the loan is set up like a line of credit, when you pay down on the loan, it does not revolve. This means that if you run into a cash shortage, you cannot draw against this loan without creating a new note subject to the approval of your banker.

RECEIVABLES

Since receivables have a cost, you should do everything in your power to accelerate the collection of outstanding receivables. If there is no cost to not paying a payable, then the incentive is not to pay it. You should therefore offer a discount to slow-paying clients for paying within 10 days of receipt of their invoice. This is effective only if it is net by 30 days and there is an interest or service charge for payment past 30 days.

Your clients have their own cash flow concerns. Unfortunately, if not handled correctly, this translates into slow receivable collection by you. Most A/E firms do not like tacking on service charges for late payment. They are afraid of losing a client if they press too hard or charge a service fee on a past due bill. And developers and other clients know this. We have even known clients owing bills 90 or more days past due that call up and have the audacity to threaten to take their business elsewhere because the secretary asked them if they could make a payment on their account.

There is grave danger in this type of attitude. Up to a certain point, the architect or engineer has a hold on the client until the work is completed and the plans are sealed and delivered. We have known A/E firms that had $100,000+ receivables go into chapter 11 bankruptcy. There is honestly no excuse for this. As a matter of practice, a client should be at least current through the last billing cycle before the final work is delivered.

This brings us to billing methods. There are many firms that do not bill a client until the project is completed. Many architectural firms send a bill to a client only after a phase is 100 percent completed. This could represent as much as three months' work before a bill is sent. It is our recommendation that a bill be sent each and every month for the amount of work performed up to that point. If it is a flat fee contract, the percentage of any phase should be calculated and billed out along with accompanying receivables.

This also has the advantage of determining the credit worthiness of the client. Most architects and engineers do not do credit checks on clients. Even if they did, the credit worthiness of a client can sometimes change virtually overnight. The best credit check is a client who pays his bills. If you wait several months before sending a bill, you may not have sufficient warning that a client is in trouble until it is too late for both of you.

Most of you are probably saying that you know all of this and do try to collect receivables. How you collect them should be addressed at the outset of the contract or negotiations, not at the time you have to collect. It should be firmly understood exactly how the client is to be billed and when you expect your money. The terms and costs of not paying on a timely basis should be well understood. Thus you will not be the one embarrassed when the client does not pay and you ask for the money. If all this is handled correctly, you should have no problem. You will have a problem if, without having discussed billing thoroughly ahead of time, you suddenly decide to penalize the client for not paying. The client then has a right to become insulted because you have obviously told him that he is no longer a preferred customer since he does not pay his bills.

PAYABLES

Payables are the other side of the cash flow coin. These are the bills you have to pay. It goes without saying that if you do not pay your bills, you will have more money to keep. Other vendors are more callous in collecting their money than are most architects and engineers, however, and they tend to charge penalties to those that do not pay. You must therefore benefit more from keeping the money while still paying the penalty than you do by paying on time.

In order to properly manage payables, you should arrange them according to due dates so that you can pay the earliest first. This is known as aging payables. It is not the same as aging receivables (a list differentiating between receivables that are current, and those that are 30, 60, or 90 or more days past due). It is simply a way to schedule payments.

It is imperative that a cash flow projection be made each month from this payables report. In this way you can see exactly how much cash is required to meet your current obligations. When preparing this report remember that you are to account for all payables, even those that are not expenses. This means that loan repayments that would normally not be considered expenses should be included on the cash flow projection report. If necessary, you should choose carefully to pay those that incur the highest penalty.

REIMBURSABLES

Do you charge a fee for handling reimbursable expenses and consultants, or do you just pass them through at cost to your clients? There is more to lose than just the potential profit of the multiplier you add on and there is a cost of handling the reimbursable which should be absorbed. But there is also a hidden cost to the reimbursable expense.

This is especially true if you have to pay for the reimbursable before you receive the money from your client. Many A/E professionals do not pay their consultants until their clients pay them. This can become a serious problem if you have a severely delinquent client.

Therefore you should factor the cost of these reimbursable

items somewhere in your fee, either as a multiplier to the reimbursable or in the fee structure itself. Remember all costs have to be recaptured or they come off the top and you pay.

Handling cash flow is an important job that must be constantly monitored. You should have the proper tools to do the job consistently. Remember, when the cash is gone, the game is over.

Payroll Costs

Without a doubt the killer expense for most firms is payroll. As we have discussed previously, this is the one expense on which you are taxed extensively in both obvious and hidden taxes as well as other hidden costs. The amount of money you pay in payroll-related taxes and other costs can amount to as little as 11 percent or as much as 18 percent. Percentagewise this is one of the highest taxes, next to corporate income tax, that your firm will pay.

There are other hidden costs related to payroll that are not so obvious. The laws and the record keeping for payroll are so complicated and the reporting so extensive to the various agencies from state to state that you cannot treat payroll in your record keeping as simply another expense. There are, of course, entire computer programs designed primarily to handle payroll. There are also firms that make a very good living doing payroll for companies. Clients will pay incredible sums just to have the worry and pain of payroll record keeping taken off their hands.

The more you shift payroll expenses to other types or classifications of expenses, the more money you will save. Let us look at the effect of the various costs of payroll and their related expenses.

The most direct cost of payroll is the matching FICA. This tax is a direct tax on the employer. The rate is roughly tied to the amount withheld from the employee, and there is what is known as the FICA limit.

In round figures, let us say that the FICA rate is 8 percent with a limit of $50,000. What this means is that you must deduct 8 percent of an employee's salary for his FICA contribution and you must contribute another 8 percent until the employee earns $50,000 in one year. What many individuals do not know is that they are not required to withhold any FICA from the employee's salary. The employer's responsibility is 16 percent. The employer is permitted by law to withhold up to a maximum of 8 percent. What this means is that if an employer wishes, he may give some employees a net check bonus, which we have found very common. The employer may elect to pay the FICA tax on behalf of the employee. There is one little quirk in the law. You must report this FICA contribution that you made on behalf of the employee as part of his gross earnings.

This brings us to another hidden or not so hidden cost to payroll and that is the penalties. Without any statistical data to back this statement up, we have found that more of our clients pay penalties to the IRS because of payroll than any other single purpose. The second most common penalty is the failure to deposit on a timely basis.

As your payrolls proceed throughout the month, you incur larger and larger obligations for the amounts of money you have withheld from your employees. This money must be deposited in a bank authorized to accept payroll withholding deposits. The timing of these deposits depends on the amount of money owed at any point in time. You must deposit at the end of the quarter, at the end of the month, or, if you owe substantial sums, within three banking days following the payroll.

Most of our clients are what are known as three-day depositors. If they fail to make this deposit within the three days allotted, they are subject to a tremendous penalty plus interest. To show you how vicious this penalty is and how uncompassionate the IRS can be concerning regulations, let us give you a short case history.

We had a large client that, through an honest oversight, forgot to make a deposit. In fact it did not come to their attention until three months after they did their quarterly reports. They honestly reported the obligation and indicated that they had made the deposit. They were contacted by the IRS and informed that the money had not been recorded. An audit was performed on their records and, sure enough, they owed the money, which they promptly sent in. They knew that they would have a penalty for not making timely deposits and that they would owe some interest on the amount not deposited on time. What they were not prepared for was the additional penalty of failure to make the deposit. When they contacted the IRS they were informed that after a certain period of time there were two distinct penalties assessed. The first was for not making the deposit and the second was for not making the deposit on time. As incredible as this sounds, the company had to pay both penalties and interest in the amount of over $3,000. Furthermore they were informed that if they did not pay the penalties and interest, there would be additional penalties and interest assessed. Of course the IRS could close the business down and seize the assets of the business and possibly the personal assets of the owners.

Therefore it is very important to recognize that the costs of payroll can grow enormously if you incur penalties by not following the rules and making your deposits and reports in a timely manner.

The next most expensive tax for the employer is the state unemployment tax. This tax can range anywhere from a low fraction of 1 percent of the employee's salary to several percentage points. The cruel part of this tax is that the rate is dependent only in part on the actions of the employer. Employers are not taxed equally, but on an experience rate of collection of unemployment insurance by employees no longer employed by the company. Generally the more claims there are, the higher the rate the employer must pay in subsequent years.

Many people are under the misconception that ex-employees can collect unemployment insurance only if they are fired or laid off. This is not true. It is very common for husbands or wives to simply follow their spouses who have been transferred to another area and thus quit their jobs and collect unemployment insurance in the new area.

The laws concerning unemployment insurance differ from state to state and constantly change with new legislation. Also the employer is subject to the economic conditions of the state and country. This is reflected in a companion tax called FUTA, which is the federal equivalent of the state unemployment tax. Although its rate is substantially below that of the state tax, it is tied very closely to it.

This tax can be devastating because of the hidden penalty that can be incurred—probably the most common penalty issued by the federal government. Virtually every firm of any size will be caught in this trap at least once.

The problem with the FUTA tax is that there are no quarterly reports to file. The only time that you think of or are even aware of the FUTA tax is when you get your form at the end of the year. When you fill out the form you may be shocked to find out that you owe a penalty for not making timely deposits.

What many firms are not aware of is that even though they

are not required to report quarterly, they are required to make deposits on a timely basis in accordance with the rules in effect at any given time.

As a final insult, the annual form is so structured that you are penalized on your FUTA tax if you did not make all of your state tax payments on a timely basis.

Workmen's compensation insurance is required in many states. If you do not carry this type of insurance, you might be forced to post a bond and become self-insured. Since this is an insurance program, the premiums are based partially on what is known as your experience rate of claims from your employees. The other part of the premium is based directly on your payroll.

The way most insurance companies work is that they ask you to fill out an application listing the types of employees you have and what the estimated annual salary of each of these will be. The company then sets an estimated premium. At the end of the year, it either gives you a form to fill out or sends someone in person to audit your payroll reports. Then the premium is actually set, based on the exact payroll paid the previous year. You then receive an adjustment in the form of a bill for monies owed or a refund.

Not only is the premium tied directly to the payroll itself, dollar for dollar, but it is based on the type of payroll employee that you maintain. Each state ranks certain job classifications at a different rate, depending on exposure to and experience in job-related accidents. For example, a secretary in the office would have a substantially lower rate applied than would a construction worker. Be careful how you classify your employees. Find out ahead of time the rate applied to each of the classifications that you report. A simple mistake in classifying an architect as a construction manager can cost you a great deal of money.

Another payroll-related expense may be one type of liability insurance policy. Many insurers use payroll as a basis for determining the premium. Recognize this and know exactly how the premiums are determined.

It goes without saying that anything you can do to diminish this killer expense will be in your best interest. Of course the IRS recognizes this as well and severe laws and penalties have been passed in order to discourage people from calling payroll expenses something else in order to evade taxes. Of course that has not stopped many employers from trying to do just that. Let us caution you that it is easier to pay the taxes than to face the ire of the IRS if you get caught breaking the law. Even if you simply make a mistake or do something out of ignorance of the rules, the penalties that you will incur are incredible. Therefore it is our recommendation that you abide by the laws and regulations at all times as they may apply.

One of the most common tactics used by A/E companies in order to reduce the effects of payroll taxes is to call their employees contract labor. They even have the audacity to include this classification in their chart of accounts, which makes it easy for the IRS to identify the infraction during an audit.

The problem is that it is very difficult to hire a draftsman, for instance, and for that individual to be truly a contract employee. Even if you hire one for a single project for a temporary period, he is still an employee: part-time and temporary are not the criteria for contract labor. You should consult your attorney or accountant in order to determine whether you are within the law when you designate certain people as contract employees.

You are generally on safe ground if the person has his own company and you are not his only client. Then, of course, you can contract drafting out to him on a regular basis. By the same token, any expense that can be taken out of the payroll area and put in contract labor will be to your advantage.

If you are using temporary employees, you are, in effect, guaranteeing layoff at the end of the project. This is especially true with clerical workers. You therefore run the risk of increasing your state unemployment insurance rate at the end of the tenure. A more prudent method is to use a temporary employment service. Even though you may pay a few dollars per hour more, you save in several ways. First, you do not have the interviewing and employment costs incurred in hiring your own temporary employees. Second, you pay no payroll costs, thereby saving about 11 to 15 percent in payroll taxes. Third, you are not subject to the other benefits, such as vacation, sick leave, insurance, pension plan, and so forth.

One growth industry that is becoming popular with many companies is the employment company that will actually hire your employees and contract them back to you. These companies also handle all of your payroll problems, write the payroll checks, handle the bookkeeping, and so on. The cost to you is the payroll itself plus whatever the company needs in order to provide the benefits and the taxes, and, of course, to make a profit.

It is not cheaper than doing it yourself, but it does free you from the worry of payroll. These employment companies may also provide your employees with additional benefits at very little cost to you because of the economy of scale at which they work. You should understand, however, exactly what the costs are and the benefits these types of companies can provide before you decide on this course.

One of the easiest ways to channel a large amount of money into nonpayroll expense concerns the payroll of the owner. Since you own the company, you can determine how much you pay yourself in payroll. Consult your accountant and attorney on how much you should pay yourself, the manner in which you should bring money out of your company, and how you should organize your company. Check, for instance, into the advantages of a subchapter S corporation. The manner in which you bring money out of your company can either increase or reduce your tax liability.

Manufacturing firms found out years ago that machines were cheaper in the long run than human beings. Under previous tax laws, the government actually paid the employer a fee for hiring machines. This was called the investment tax credit. In addition, any expenses concerning these machines were classified as ordinary expenses as opposed to payroll expenses.

Another advantage to using a machine instead of a person is that during a business slowdown, the machine does not continue to incur a payroll cost. There are no layoffs or other human considerations. You do not have to provide vacation or sick leave benefits or cover the machine under your hospital or pension plan.

Although we are being facetious here, the fact of the matter is that A/E firms have the ability to take advantage of the automation and technology that is growing by leaps and bounds today. CAD is becoming incredibly affordable. It has the potential, through its increase in productivity, of not only replacing drafting personnel, but also allowing the designer, architect, and engineer to work smarter and faster so that not as many employees are needed to put out the same amount of work.

One consideration of automation in the A/E office is that the machine does not require a periodic review with an accompanying raise every six months to a year. This is another hidden cost of employees. The more experience an employee has with your firm, the more valuable he is to you. Thus if you want to keep this employee you must give periodic raises. These raises do not always reflect a comparable increase in productivity or value on the part of the employee that justifies the increase in salary, not to mention all the related taxes and other costs discussed.

Therefore, when you are evaluating the cost of automation in the A/E office, you should take into consideration not only the cost versus productivity increase that is available, but also the tax savings relating to the shifting of the same expenditures to ordinary costs from payroll, including the effect of layoffs on unemployment insurance during an economic downturn.

And finally there are minor ways you can shift potential payroll costs to ordinary ones. This is in the area of employee benefits. There are several areas of the law permitting employee benefits that are ordinary expenses to the company and nontaxable benefits to the employee. Some of these might include health and life insurance, other forms of medical insurance, and so on. Of course the IRS and Congress are trying to close down as many of these as possible, so first check current laws and regulations.

We strongly recommend that you consult an accountant to review your payroll policies and your corporate, partnership, or personal business organization to see if payroll expenses can be diminished under current laws and regulations. This type of consultation will usually more than pay for itself.

Budgeting

Most people think of budgeting as a method of limiting spending. Although that is part of budgeting, it is not the primary purpose. One of the ways of expanding a business is to spend money. We have never met the owner of a company who has said he is in business to get smaller. Everyone wants to expand the size and especially the profitability of their company.

First let us look at the kind of budget we are going to discuss here. A/E firms use many types of budgets, for instance, project budgets, but here we are concerned with the financial budgets that usually accompany the general ledger's chart of accounts.

Before you can begin to develop a financial budget for your company, you must first look at the company's chart of accounts. As we discussed in another chapter, the chart of accounts is divided into five categories:

Assets
Liabilities
Capital
Revenue
Expenses

Budgets generally are not required, or recommended, for the three primary accounts: assets, liabilities, and capital. They are reserved for the capital contra accounts: revenue and expenses.

Keep in mind that you must think in terms of budgeting not only revenue but also expenses. In order to budget both revenue and expenses, you must first have a goal for your company. You need to know where your company is going in the coming year and how you want it to get there. Until you can begin to anticipate your potential revenue, you should not establish a budget. Too many firms start with the expense side of the budget to see what they want to spend, then decide that if they spend this amount they will need so much revenue to cover it. Unfortunately this is the way that "not for profit" organizations, such as the federal government, budget. They see what they need to spend and then acquire, through taxes, the revenue necessary to support the habit.

A "for profit" company should work in just the opposite manner. You should first decide what profit you wish to attain and, with this goal in mind, determine how much revenue it will take to create that kind of profit. Next you should look at the revenue to determine how much money you will have to spend in order to generate and support that kind of revenue. This becomes your company's blueprint for the upcoming year. Notice here you are using the budget not to simply limit spending but to know where that spending has to occur in order to generate the revenue necessary to create the desired net profit.

When developing your revenue budget you should follow the pattern of your general ledger for all revenue accounts. This would typically include fee income, reimbursable income, and other income. Of course it can be broken down into more categories as the needs of your organization dictate.

If you are using a computerized general ledger, make sure that the program you invest in permits the budgeting of revenue as well as of expenses. Depending on the program you will probably need to put your revenue budgets in with a negative to identify that you are budgeting a credit amount rather than a debit amount. Consult your program for the exact procedure. The end result in your budget for revenue over expenditures is that you wind up budgeting for net income or profit. In this way the total net income account should have a budgeted figure in it that represents the profit goals of the company.

Once the income is budgeted, you should turn your attention to the expense side of the ledger. Regardless of how you have organized your general ledger—fixed-variable or direct-indirect—you will have certain fixed expenses. You must identify these fixed expenses and budget for them first. Remember, this represents your fixed overhead that you must account for before you begin making a profit. Most ongoing companies have certain fixed expenses, such as their rent, over which they have very little control. If you budget these accounts first, you will be able to see exactly how much money you must make at the outset.

This total of fixed expenses should now be compared with the amount of income you are budgeting. Looking at the previous year's general ledger, you should be able to determine how much of the balance of the expense accounts are necessary percentagewise to generate $1 in revenue. If, for example, direct salaries represented a certain percentage of the overall income, that amount should be budgeted into that account. The balance of the fixed amount of your payroll should be budgeted to the indirect side. At this point you should get a percentage of direct salaries to total salaries and see what total utilization rate your company will have to maintain in order to generate the direct labor expense necessary to produce the desired income. Then see if it is reasonable.

Each of the variable expenses should be identified in this manner and budgeted as a percentage of the projected income. What you are trying to do is to set the variable expenses at a reasonable percentage of the revenue that they are intended to support. In doing so, as your revenue goes up or declines, you can adjust the budget for these accounts to reflect the same percentage difference.

Finally look at the tax-related expenses. Each tax is based on something. Personal property tax might be based on assets, for example, and payroll taxes on payroll. Therefore each of these accounts should have budgets that reflect the amount of taxes that would have to be paid based on the budgets of the related accounts.

After adding up all the budgeted accounts for both revenue and expenditures, you will come out with a budgeted net income. This income will be either above or below the goal that you set for the company at the outset. If below you must adjust the budgets either for additional revenue or for cuts in the expenditures. In the unlikely event that you have too much net profit, you should look at the budget and see if it is reasonable.

The process of budgeting is not scientifically based. There are some procedures, but basically budgeting is a give-and-take, trial-and-error process. Remember that a budget is a blueprint for the success of your company. It is also an ongoing measurement of how your company is reaching its predetermined goals, and because of this it is not enough to measure how you are doing once a year. By the time the year is over, it is too late. Then what we are talking about is a postmortem, not a tool for management decisions.

Therefore it is essential that the budgets for the various accounts be further divided into monthly budgets and possibly quarterly budgets. Money is neither earned nor spent on an annual basis. Money is earned and spent day-by-day and month-by-month. The month and quarter are natural measuring points throughout the year.

Nothing extraordinary is required to determine the monthly or quarterly budgets. Once you have the annual budgets, you may simply want to divide by 12 for the monthly and by 4 for the quarterly. Of course we all know that money is not made or spent that equally, so you might want to do a little more work and create a budget for each quarter or month. Just make sure that all 12 months or all 4 quarters add up to the sum total of the annual budget.

Once you have your budget designed and the year begins, you are ready to evaluate the progress of your company. There are three basic pieces of information you should look for in the budgets you have prepared. The first is the percentage of revenue that has come in or the percentage of the budget that you have expended. This is a percentage measurement of how close you are to coming in on budget, whether it be revenue or expenditures.

If you are measuring the monthly or quarterly budgets, you should do so at the end of the month or the quarter if you want a true picture of your success or failure. If you have not budgeted monthly or quarterly—only annually—the information you get will represent the percentage spent and will have to be interpreted in relation to the percentage of the year that has passed.

Another measurement is in constant dollars that you have left. This is simply a subtraction exercise. It is this measurement that is used primarily in not for profit companies. They are faced with legal limits on spending and it is imperative that they do not exceed their budgets in specified accounts. Therefore it is helpful to know what the balance left to be expended is at all times.

This is of limited interest to for profit companies but can be a useful curiosity feature. The problem with knowing how much money you have left to spend is the same trap that the government falls into—you begin to feel you must spend it.

The third measurement is used to analyze accounts in relationship to their percentage of income. Remember this is how you began your budgeting process for variable expenses. So it makes sense to keep an eye on these variables to monitor their percentage relationship and to make sure they are not getting out of hand. This can be one of the first indications that you need to take a good hard look at your billing rates.

Remember that the purpose of a financial budget is not to limit spending. It is to give you a financial tool to create a blueprint for the financial goals of your company. It is this tool that permits you to monitor the activities of your company as it progresses. Without this monitoring process you are wasting your time with budgets. The budget gives you the information necessary to set goals for your company and to see how it is progressing toward those goals.

One word of caution. Do not use the budget as a straitjacket that inhibits the growth of your company. The government by law has to use its budget to control public spending. Remember, however, that your budget is for your use as a monitoring device. So the next time you say that it is not in the budget, recognize that it can be put in the budget. Use the budget to recognize the effects of expenditures, not to inhibit growth.

Hidden Costs

In previous chapters we have touched on hidden costs as they relate to payroll expenses in the form of penalties. But there are hidden costs at virtually every turn.

How many times, for example, have you gone to buy a car and known in your heart that you will have to pay substantially more than the price agreed upon before you are finished. Then there are the costs of buying a house. Not even the real estate agent can tell you to the penny how much you will have to spend at closing.

These are two types of hidden costs, but there are more. There are those costs that are not actually part of the original sale, and, unfortunately, they are almost impossible to budget for. But you must be aware of them so you can properly evaluate the wisdom of a given purchase. Let us now take a look at some kinds (and these are by no means all) of hidden costs.

INTEREST

It is easy enough to compute the interest expense on expansion loans. It is the effect of the interest on the line of credit that is difficult to manage. Remember that the purpose of the line of credit is to replace the cash that is not available because of receivables (it is, in fact, the most evident cost of receivables). Of course, even if you have the cash resources to operate and thus cover the receivables yourself, you are missing the earning power of the capital that you could have kept in savings or money market accounts.

What is not so evident is the dilution of your balance sheet. Even though you have increased liabilities and assets by the exact same dollar amount, you have changed your ratio of current assets to current liabilities. You have also diluted your borrowing power and credit line. This has the potential of translating itself into lost opportunities and diminished future revenue: If you had the cash available, you possibly could do more marketing or even take advantage of cash discounts. The result is that there is a cost that is not measurable but at the same time very real.

SERVICE CHARGES

Service charges are akin to interest in that they represent the use of money. These could be bank service charges or late charges on your payables. Again this has the potential of being tied back to the timely collection of your receivables.

What you have to watch is the annual interest rate you are paying. One of the reasons that most firms choose to call it a service charge as opposed to interest on past due is that true interest is subject to state usury laws. Service charges, on the other hand, can include not only the interest on past due but also the internal cost of handling a delinquent account.

We have seen some service charges as high as 60 percent APR (annual percentage rate—an interest calculation method). If these service charges are not paid, some companies will charge a service charge on the unpaid amount, which can amount to substantial sums.

INSURANCE

Insurance is a necessary expense for the protection of a company. But too many companies are either drastically underinsured or shamelessly overinsured.

In most states it is illegal to collect more on a loss than the actual loss is worth. Therefore you should never insure anything for more than its value. In fact many states permit you to insure for as little as 80 percent of the current value and the insurance company will replace the full value of the loss.

The point is that insurance is a gamble. You are betting that you are going to have a loss and therefore are willing to pay a little now so that you will not have to pay a lot later. The insurance company is betting that you will not have a loss and therefore would like to keep your premium.

There are many things that affect the cost of the premium. The biggest is the deductible. This is the amount that you are willing to risk without insurance. The higher the deductible expenses, the lower the premium.

This is where the hidden cost is. If you have a good record and rarely have a loss, it is to your advantage to have a high deductible. In effect, you become the co-insurer. If you have a relatively low deductible, however, the difference in the premiums is the hidden cost if you do not have the claims to justify it.

This is true with any insurance policy. When deciding on which insurance premium to choose, therefore, you should always calculate the cost of the deductible variable. By doing so you can actually save substantial amounts of money.

We are not encouraging you to always decide on high deductible limits. We just want you to calculate the cost of the additional insurance you are buying for the lower deductible and see if the additional premium is warranted for the particular situation.

PENALTIES

Most of the penalties you are going to have to pay will be related to taxes. We have already discussed in detail the various penalties that can be incurred relating to payroll. But there are other tax penalties that are lurking in the wings. These penalties can be for almost anything. They might be for failure to file a personal property tax rendition. They could be related to sales taxes. Unfortunately, most of the time you are not forewarned of the penalty or the amount of the penalty until it is assessed.

In some states, even if you owe no money, failure to file a report can subject you to penalties involving incredible amounts of money. What is clear here is that you should know the laws and the regulations of your particular state. Our philosophy is that it isn't what you know that can hurt you, it's what you don't know.

AFTER COSTS

These are costs that occur after the sale. These would include additional personnel costs, consultant costs, or supplies. We have found that most major costs require additional support costs. Although there is nothing wrong with after costs—they are usually necessary expenses—you should know they exist and factor them in when you are making a decision concerning a proposed expenditure.

PRICE CHANGES

This is the most elusive of the hidden costs because a price change can occur in either direction. How many times have you bought something only to see it on sale the next week? Obviously you were a victim of the hidden cost: You bought too early. But also how many times have you waited to make a decision only to find that there was a price increase or that the sale had expired.

Obviously, if you could always predict prices, you could make more money in the financial markets than in your particular business. At the same time, you can usually see whether the product you are anticipating purchasing is in an inflationary cycle or a deflationary one.

The problem here is that a deflationary cycle can be more dangerous and filled with an even more devastating hidden cost than an inflationary cycle. In an inflationary cycle, the only thing that can hurt you is the little bit more, or even the lot more, that you may have to pay for a product. But in a deflationary cycle, the temptation is too great to wait and not make a decision on a product you need in hopes that the price will decline further.

Your decision should not be made on the price of a product alone. If your company can make substantial sums of money by purchasing a product, then that product either is cost effective at a given price or it is not. If it is, you should buy it *now*. Waiting will mean that you will not have the opportunity to improve your profitability because you are standing around waiting for the opportune price. You could wait forever. So what if you pay a little too much. It will either make you money or it will not. Evaluate a product primarily on need and not on price. Although price should be considered, it is secondary to your need for the product.

We honestly believe that companies do better in an inflationary cycle because at that point they are afraid of waiting and being left behind as prices rise.

COSTS OF SERVICE

Here we are not talking about repair service but about product support and training after the sale.

When you purchase a television set, you would not pay an

additional fee for someone to tell you how to operate it. But computers, for example, are another story. Because of the sophistication of these machines—and often the mystery that surrounded them—the fear of buying one of the most expensive paperweights on earth at one time forced many A/E professionals to pay an enormous price for service and support that they may or may not have received. It was also difficult to determine just how much they were paying for this support because it was so well hidden in the price; it was never separated out.

But now, with the advent of discount computer stores and mail-order computer houses, the client can see just how much profit was built in for this support. We are not telling you to get all of your equipment from a discount mail-order house, but there are now many people who really know what they are doing, and most of them are not in the computer stores. Computers have also been around long enough now that most firms have people on their staff who know how to format a disk and do backups. With the decline of the "full service" computer stores in favor of the specialized application dealers, the client is at least getting more value for the support he is paying for.

You should pay only for the services that you want and need, and look for hidden costs for service that you probably do not need and may not get. See how much you can get the equipment for as a "box"; that is, just a computer in a box—no service, support, or maintenance, and maybe even "some assembly required." Then decide on the level of service you need and how much that is going to cost. You will then be in a better position to decide if you wish to purchase the computer.

SERVICE CONTRACTS

The service contract is for repair, generally for parts and labor. Regardless of how this is sold, it is an insurance policy, and therefore has all of the pros and cons of one. In deciding on whether to purchase the policy, you should evaluate the service record and needs of the product. If it is a product that rarely breaks down, you might think twice about the contract. If it does have a high failure rate, the policy might be an advantageous purchase.

There are two additional factors you should consider when

deciding on whether to take on a service contract. The first is the availability of the service if you do not have a contract. There are many firms that will guarantee a level of service, such as 6, 24, or 48 hours. Naturally you pay more for the better response time. What is implied here is that if you do not have a service contract, service response time is going to depend on how many service contract holders in need of service are ahead of you. This may incur a hidden cost that could be very expensive in the long run.

The second factor is that having a service contract permits you to control all costs so you do not have any surprises. You will be able to budget all costs related to the purchase and operation of the equipment.

DOWN TIME

When you choose to automate your office you tend to become very dependent on the new equipment. In fact, many automated A/E firms cannot imagine how they could possibly operate on manual systems.

For companies that have come to depend on automation, any disruption in this procedure costs money, so backup systems should be put in place beforehand. Down time is very expensive.

As we said in the beginning, hidden costs are everywhere. Although we have not made an attempt to isolate hidden costs in every situation, we have attempted to illustrate where they might be found. You, in turn, should train yourself to look for them in your evaluation of a proposed expense so that you can have as much information as possible beforehand.

Internal Controls

The subject of internal controls is a touchy one. The primary purpose of internal controls is to prevent theft, a subject we do not want to think about. We would rather make the assumption that all of our employees are part of the family and that they would never steal. But some people are dishonest. If you say that you are in no danger of theft from employees, ask yourself if you would mind giving every employee on your staff unlimited signature and borrowing power in your name.

The purpose of this chapter is to let you know where the holes are so that you can establish the controls to plug them up. There is of course a cost to internal controls. As with an insurance policy, you spend the money in order to protect yourself from a possible greater loss.

The security arrangements and precautions taken by a large bank are not the same as those needed by a six-person A/E firm, since your exposure to possible loss is not the same as a bank's. However, the larger you get and the more employees you have the greater your exposure. In other words, the more you have to steal and the more people there are in a position to steal, the more protection you will need. What you must do is to take a survey of your exposure and what you have to protect. This analysis should include your bank accounts, how much money is kept where, who has signature power, limitations, and so on.

WHY EMPLOYEES STEAL

Believe it or not, most embezzlers believe that they are basically honest people and would never steal from anyone. Most thefts occur for two reasons. First, the employee has overwhelming personal financial problems and there is no other place to turn. As a result he "borrows" the funds necessary with the true belief at the time that he will pay the money back. Once he discovers the ease with which this solves his problems, it occurs more than once. Of course this individual is never able to repay the "debt" and simply continues with the thefts.

The second reason involves the disgruntled employee. This

is an employee who rationalizes that he deserves the stolen money because of the things he has done for the company that have gone unrewarded. He might be resentful because his salary is too low or because he feels he has no opportunity for promotion and advancement.

Let us look at a couple of the more common methods of theft that have been used in the past.

The Dummy Company

The object of this theft is to write what appear to be legitimate checks for merchandise that was not delivered. In this way the money is properly accounted for and does not appear to be missing from the books.

It requires that the person authorizing the payments for the delivered goods set up a dummy company, which issues your company an invoice. Therefore the invoice matches your purchase order system and is paid. The check is cashed and the books balance. The only things missing are the goods or services that were purchased. A variation on this theme involves using real companies and colluding with them to overbill the company for services that were not performed.

This type of theft can go on indefinitely because the books balance, and unless there is a physical check or a comparison of departments and productivity, it is difficult to catch.

Dummy Reports

This is a rather straightforward theft. It occurs when there are substantial funds in CDs or money market accounts that are not needed for current obligations.

If the individual that has signatory power is the same person that has the responsibility of reporting the financial condition of the company, it is a simple case of drawing out the money. Generally it does not matter who the checks are written to. Often a separate account will be set up. Money may be transferred by telephone from legitimate accounts to the special account this individual has set up in the company's name. The bank may not find anything unusual about this arrangement because there are many firms that have multiple demand accounts.

The key to this system is to continue to report the balances of the CDs as they are supposed to be. This method of embezzlement cannot go on indefinitely, however. Eventually, even with a rudimentary company audit, it will be caught.

The money is often stolen rather rapidly prior to a vacation. This gives the individual two uninterrupted weeks before anyone begins to look for him. This type of theft is sometimes unrecoverable and is a total loss to the company even if the individual is caught and sent to jail.

There are many more ways that theft can occur, but it is not the purpose of this book to teach you how people can steal from you. What we want to stress is how you can protect yourself from potential theft using rudimentary methods of control.

PREVENTING THEFT

Signature Authority

Who has signature authority over your checking accounts? For convenience you may want to give signature authority to several people. If this is the case, you should consider requiring that two signatures be on the checks. This is something that most firms are aware of and generally do. What is unfortunate is that they feel this is all that is necessary to be protected.

The plain truth is that a check has about a 90 percent chance of going through a bank with the name Mickey Mouse on it. You can imagine how effective a rudimentary attempt at forgery would be. You might want to consider check amount limits for certain employees. This would give you the convenience of not having to be bothered with small checks but at the same time would limit your exposure to substantial losses. Remember this is a minimal control. It is not even close to foolproof.

Lock Up Your Checks

This is a minor precaution that does not cost you anything but should be considered because the more banks automate, the less they can protect you from unauthorized use of your checks. Many times checks are stolen from the bottom and are not discovered for months.

Diversify Responsibility

The individual with the authority to balance and reconcile the checkbooks should not have the ability to sign checks. This is a routine diversification of responsibility, and the more diversified the responsibility the more protection you have. You can spread this safeguard to all levels, from the issuance of purchase orders to the final approval for release of checks. Of course you must be reasonable. A small firm with only six employees cannot diversify the responsibilities as much as a major corporation can.

Account for Voided Checks

You should have a system of voiding checks both in the checkbook and on the records. Keep all copies of voided checks for audit purposes so that they can be accounted for at all times.

Perform a Proof of Cash

This is an audit term and is intended to discourage temporary "borrowing" from the company. The easiest way to discourage theft is to let the employees know that there are good controls in the company. The proof of cash is a very good deterrent.

You simply check the bank balance at the end of a given time with the book balance for the same period and reconcile. What you are looking for are any delays in deposits that might show a pattern. The discrepancy can work both ways. Deposits made to the bank in months in which they are not booked can show up repayments from "borrowing." This procedure should be undertaken on a periodic basis by individuals not responsible for making deposits or reconciling the books.

Pay By Invoice

This control does not have as much to do with eliminating internal theft as it does with just good business practice. It is a simple technique, but it can save your company a lot of money.

There are two types of bills that your company will receive: the invoice and the statement. There is nothing wrong with statements. They are good for both companies to use to help balance their invoices.

But you should never pay by statement. The problem is that it is very difficult to identify exactly what you are paying for.

Many companies pay both from statement and invoice. An invoice is a single bill for an item or group of items purchased at one time. If you pay only from invoices, your chances of double payments are greatly reduced.

When an invoice is paid, a copy should be attached to your copy of the check. In this way if there is ever doubt about whether something has been paid, you will have a confirming copy. If a vendor says that you owe additional money, you simply ask for a duplicate invoice for the unpaid amounts.

Although it is a very simple concept, you would be amazed at the number of companies that continue to pay from whatever comes in. It is difficult for them to maintain control over anything that is paid.

Purchase Order System

A purchase order system is usually not recommended for small firms because of the additional cost incurred. But for larger firms, it becomes essential to control purchases and to try to maintain control on purchase authorizations.

The concept of a purchase order system is quite simple. The purchase order is, at minimum, a three-part form: one for the vendor, one for the business office, and one for the originator.

The procedure is as follows. Once a purchase is to be made, the purchase order is filled out and approved by someone in authority to approve the spending. The approved purchase order is then sent to the business office, where it is recorded. The original is sent to the vendor to order the merchandise and a copy is returned to the individual making the purchase. One copy is maintained by the business office as an outstanding obligation.

The business office waits for two items before it can make a payment to the vendor. First, it must receive an invoice that matches the purchase order. Then, when the goods come in, the originator signs his copy of the purchase order and returns this copy to the business office. This authorization says that the goods that were ordered are in and payment is approved.

Remember that the business office must have both the invoice from the vendor and the authorization copy of the purchase order from the purchaser before a check can be cut. If one comes in without the other, it is simply clipped to the business office copy of the purchase order until the other item comes in.

Once the paperwork is complete and the check has been written, the authorization copy of the purchase, the invoice, and a copy of the check are attached and eventually put in the permanent business file. This division of authorization adds a higher degree of control because the system is meant to diversify the purchaser from the authorizer and to provide independent confirmation by invoice from the vendor.

As we mentioned earlier, not every company needs this amount of control. As you can see there is a cost involved, not only in money but in increased bureaucracy. A simpler purchase order system for a smaller firm would be to simply write down on a form, numbered if you wish, what it is that you ordered and put it in an envelope. Match the form with the invoice when it comes in. When it is paid, file it with the appropriate records.

This second method is not a true purchase order system but is the minimum necessary to keep track of what has been ordered and what has not.

The Outside Audit

This is not as awesome as it may sound. What it simply means is that you have a CPA firm come in once a year to do a cursory audit. What is involved is a sampling of checks at random to make sure they have all the paperwork necessary. Checks are also traced back through the general ledger entries to confirm that they were properly recorded to the right accounts. Other samplings are done, and a proof of cash is performed for perhaps two months of the year.

The purpose of the outside audit is not to uncover some earth-shattering theft that might be operating in your business; it is to discourage honest employees from becoming dishonest.

As we said at the beginning, the extent of internal controls are directly dependent on the size of the firm and the exposure to loss. The only admonition that we would like to make is that you should not take internal controls for granted. As your firm grows, keep in mind that the degree of internal controls must grow also.

Conclusion

Cost management is not a part-time job. There are only two ways that you can increase the profitability of your company. One way is to increase your business and thus your revenue. The other way is to cut expenses. It is of course elementary to say that the net profits of a company are the difference between the two.

Unfortunately most firms spend all of their energy trying to increase the profitability of the company simply by increasing revenues. Although this is an admirable task and should not be ignored, the techniques discussed in this section can have equally rewarding outcomes.

The techniques described here may or may not be for you. Use those that are applicable and feel free to adapt the concepts to your particular company and needs.

GLOSSARY

Accounts Payable: The process of accounting for monies owed. It is generally incorporated in an accounts payable program, which accounts for invoices billed to the A/E firm and writes checks to vendors owed.

Adjusted Budget: The modification of a project budget according to the current job cost rate, in which the dollar cost remains fixed and the available hours are modified.

Advertising: That part of marketing that notifies clients about services you provide.

A/E: The industries of architecture, engineering, and design.

Alternate of Choice: A question you ask a client that gives him a choice of two alternatives, both of which are acceptable to you. It must not be a yes or no question.

Billing Rate: The dollar rate at which each hour is to be billed to the client.

Break-even: In manufacturing and merchandising, the point at which the profit on all existing sales is equal to fixed expenses. In A/E firms the income necessary for break-even is (Indirect Expenses/Overhead Rate)(Overhead Rate + 1).

Brochure: A pamphlet describing your firm and the services that you can provide.

Budget: A predetermined limit you do not want to exceed. It may be a dollar budget in the general ledger accounts, a budget for dollars or time in job costing, or a dollar budget in billing.

Capitalize: To account for an expenditure as an asset. Later the asset is expensed according to a schedule to spread the cost of the expenditure over a greater period of time.

Circular E: A federal bulletin that contains the schedules for payroll and FICA withholdings.

Classification: The job title or duties of an employee.

Closing: The procedure by which you attempt to get the client to agree to use your services.

Comp Time: Compensatory time or time that is worked but not paid. Generally comp time is given as time off in the future for overtime that is worked.

Consultants: Individuals or businesses that bill out their services to you and are not part of your payroll.

Contract Labor: Employees of short duration employed for specific projects. The term is often used to evade payroll taxes by removing these individuals from the official payroll. The IRS and other government agencies have specific guidelines concerning use and accounting of contract labor.

Corporation: A legal entity chartered by a state to conduct business. A corporation is comprised of stockholders. The corporation is generally the entity, not the individual stockholders, and is taxed as such.

Cost Analysis Survey: A survey instrument used to evaluate the need and cost/benefit ratio of a projected expenditure. It is used primarily to evaluate competing expenditures.

Cost Estimating: The process of deriving costs for the purpose of creating a budget of hours and dollars available to you to perform on a fixed fee project.

Cutoff Date: The date after which no time or direct charges are accounted for, paid, or billed. This is generally used in job costing, billing, payroll, and accounts payable.

Data Base: A collection of computer records containing specific information. Each piece of information is contained in a field. The data base is managed by a computer program or data base manager.

Depreciation: The process of expensing a capitalized asset.

Direct Charges: All expenses to a project other than labor expenses and overhead. This would incluce reimburseables, nonreimbursables, and consultants.

Direct Expenses: Dollar expenses (not time) that are attributable to a project for which revenue is received. Direct expenses may or may not be reimbursable. They especially include payroll expenses attributable to projects.

Direct Mail: Contacting potential clients by mail.

Direct Time: Time that is attributable to a project for which revenue is received. It is not necessary that direct time be billable by the hour. The project may be fixed fee.

Federal Depository: A federal bank authorized to accept deposits of money withheld from employee payroll and any other federal tax money due from the employer.

FICA: Social Security tax.

Field: A subdivision of a data base record which is the smallest piece of information by which you are able to enter data or search. Fields could be name, address, zip code, and so on.

Fixed Expenses: Dollar expenses that do not fluctuate from month to month in proportion to a predetermined unit of measurement such as sales or revenue. These are the dollar expenditures necessary whether or not any revenue is generated.

Fixed Fee Project: A project for which a fee is fixed by contract or agreement regardless of the number of hours worked. Sometimes referred to as a contract or flat fee project.

Flat Fee: Same as fixed fee.

FUTA: Federal unemployment tax.

General Ledger: A series of accounts, used in accounting, to which money is posted.

Hidden Cost: An additional unanticipated cost that relates to the expenditure for something else.

Hourly to Maximum: An hourly billed project with a maximum limit. Hours worked in excess of this limit are not billed to the client.

Hourly Project: A project for which a fee is not fixed, but is based on the number of hours worked times the hourly rates of the employees or their classifications.

Hybrid Project: A project that is billed as some variation of a fixed fee project but that also bills additional services on an hourly basis.

Indirect Expenses: Dollar expenses (not time) that are not attributable to a project for which revenue is received. Indirect expenses are typically referred to as overhead.

Indirect Time: Time that is not attributable to a project for which revenue is received. This is often called administrative time, non-billable time, or overhead time.

Investment Cost: An expense that brings a return which equals or exceeds the initial investment.

Job Costing: The process of tracking all costs to a project in terms of labor, direct charges, and overhead.

Job Cost Rate: The dollar rate used to determine the cost of each hour spent on a project.

Joint Venture: Two or more individuals or entities joining for a single business purpose. Each individual or entity maintains his separate business identity during the venture. This should not be confused with a legal partnership.

Market Analysis: The process of finding out and writing down everything you can concerning potential clients, their needs, and what they are willing to pay. Market analysis also includes knowing what other A/E firms in the area are doing and the compensation they are receiving for their services.

Marketing: Advertising, public relations, market analysis, and selling.

Marketing Ratio: (Total Marketing Expenses)/(Gross Professional Revenue + Reimbursable Revenue − All direct expenses other than direct labor). This figure should be between 5 and 10 percent of the total income from professional services.

Objections: Questions asked by clients during the selling process. Although these are in the form of objecting to something they are really indications that the client is progressing and is truly interested in the services.

Overhead Rate: A ratio of direct salary expense divided by indirect expenses.

Partnership: A legal entity of two or more individuals or entities joining in a permanent single business entity.

Percentage of Construction: A variation of a fixed fee project. The fee is not actually fixed but instead is tied to a percentage of the final construction cost. In a true percentage of construction cost project the fee can fluctuate up or down, depending on the final audited costs of construction.

Percentage of Phase: A variation of a fixed fee project. The fee is divided into phases with each phase accounting for a specified percentage of the overall project. Revenue is received in accordance with the percentage completed of each phase.

Phase Task: A method of accounting for time. The phase is the highest level in the organizational hierarchy of activities and the task is the lowest. Generally tasks can be performed only within phases.

Print Advertising: Any form of printed material used specifically for advertising purposes. The term generally refers to advertising in newspapers, journals, magazines, or other print media.

Productivity Rate: The quantity of work produced divided by the available time. This is not usually used in A/E firms. It is not to be confused with the utilization rate.

Promotion: See Advertising.

Proof of Cash: An audit term that reconciles book balances with bank balances for the same period of time. It is meant to discourage "borrowing" from the company.

Prospecting: The process of contacting potential clients.

Public Relations: The part of marketing that has as its goal the projection of a good public image and reputation.

Purchase Order: A control document used to authorize purchases and payments.

Qualifying: Verifying that the potential client is able to use the A/E firm's services.

Referral: A procedure by which an existing client provides a favorable introduction to a potential client. The referral may be direct or indirect, such as permission to use a name.

Request for Proposal (RFP): A request issued by a client for A/E firms to bid (compete) for a project.

Selling: The process of getting the client to use services.

Sole Proprietorship: A single individual or entity engaged in business.
Square Foot Project: A variation of a fixed fee project. The fee is based on a dollar amount times the number of square feet of the project.
Sub Chapter S: A corporation that has elected to be taxed as a sole proprietorship or a partnership rather than as a corporation.
Telemarketing: Contacting potential clients by telephone.
Three-day Depositor: An employer whose payroll withholding debt obligation to the federal government has reached a predetermined dollar amount. In this event the employer is required to deposit that money with a Federal Depository within three banking days following the payroll.
Tickler Date: A specific type of date used as a reminder.
Time Accounting: The process of accounting for time spent. This is not to be confused with time management, which is the arranging of time to be used in the most productive manner.
Time Sheet: A form delineating the time spent for each phase task of each project. This form is used for payroll, billing, and job costing.
Utilization Rate: A ratio of direct time divided by total time. A variation of the utilization rate for salaried employees is direct time divided by available time. If it is a 40-hour week, then 40 is the available time.
Variable Expenses: Dollar expenses that fluctuate proportionately with a predetermined unit of measurement, typically sales or revenue. Variable expenses are generally tracked by manufacturing or merchandising firms. Although there is some relationship, variable expenses are not totally synonymous with direct expenses.
Variance: The percentage difference between what is budgeted and what is spent.
Work in Progress: The amount of time performed on a project that has not been billed. It is sometimes called unbilled services.

Index

Accounting
  accrual, 58, 61, 188, 192
  internal controls, 214–20
  manipulation of, 188–90
  principles of, 186–87. *See also* Chart of accounts; General ledger
Accounts payable, 58–60
Accounts receivable, 58, 59. *See also* Billing
Additional services phase, 13–14, 22–23, 57
Adjusted budget, 49
Advances, 66
Advertising, 89–90, 125–34
  direct mail, 94, 125–32
  print, 133–34
  telemarketing, 132–33
AIA, 5, 13
Audit, outside, 219–20
Automation, 12, 201–2, 213

Benefits, 73, 202
Bidding, 10–11, 40–44, 45. *See also* Project cost estimating
Billing, 50–57
  and cash flow, 193
  cut off date, 61
  flat fee, 40, 41, 46, 50, 51–57, 62
  hourly, 40–41, 46, 50, 51
  internal controls, 217–18
  percentage of construction cost, 54–56
  percentage of phase completed, 51–54
  and phase task codes, 10
  square foot, 56–57
  and time accounting, 16, 17, 22–23. *See also* Accounts receivable
Break-even analysis, 180, 181–93
Brochures, 83–84, 135–36
Budgeting, 203–7
  adjusted budget, 49
  for advertising, 134
  importance of, 169
  and phase task codes, 10–11
  and project cost estimating, 47
  for taxes, 205
Budget variance, 47–48
Buttonholing, 79–80

CAD systems, 119–20, 176, 201
Capital investment, 189
Cash management
  loans, 191–92
  payables, 194
  receivables, 192–93
  reimbursables, 194–95
Chart of accounts, 30–32, 34–35, 67–70, 178, 203. *See also* General ledger
Client billing. *See* Billing
Community involvement, 87
Compensatory time, 70–71
Competitors, information on, 115–16, 118–24
Computers, 75
  and accounts payable, 59–60
  A/E firm data base, 115–17
  and billing, 57
  and budgeting, 204
  client data base, 91, 100, 104–15
  cost of, 75, 177, 185, 212
  and direct mail advertising, 128

and historical analysis, 12
news publication data base, 138
and overhead rate, 39
and payroll, 70–71
and phase task codes, 8, 9–10, 12
and time accounting, 19, 20
and time analysis, 24–25
and work in progress, 62
Congratulatory letter, 101, 126, 129–30
Contract labor, 23, 72, 179–80, 200
Cost Analysis Survey, 171–77
Cost estimating. *See* Project cost estimating
Cost management
accounting, 186–90
cash flow, 191–95
Cost Analysis Survey, 171–77
hidden costs, 208–13
importance of, 169–70
internal controls, 214–20
payroll, 196–202
types of costs, 178–85. *See also* Budgeting
Crisscross directory, 120–21

Deductions, 66, 68, 70
Deferred assets, 189
Depreciation, 189
Direct charges, 48–49
Direct expenses, 180–83
Direct mail advertising, 114–15, 125–32
Direct mail questionnaire, 121

Embezzling, 214–16
Employee classifications, 20, 43–44, 51, 116, 199, 200
Employee leaves, 70–71
Employee number, 20
Employment companies, 200–201
Expenses
direct vs. indirect, 29, 32–33, 180–83
fixed vs. variable, 178, 179–80, 204, 205, 207
reimbursable vs. nonreimbursable, 33, 48–49, 194–95

Fact sheet, 138–39
Federal withholding tax, 65, 68
Fees, 92, 156
FICA tax, 65, 68, 71, 183, 196–97
Fixed expenditures, 178, 180, 204
Fixed fee billing. *See* Flat fee billing
Flat fee billing, 50, 51–57
and job costing, 46
and project cost estimating, 40, 41
and work in progress, 62
Follow-up, 84
FUTA tax, 71, 183, 198–99

General ledger, 29–35
and accounts payable, 60
payroll, 67–70. *See also* Accounting; Chart of accounts
Government contracts, 20

Hidden costs, 185, 196, 208–13
Historical analysis, 21, 24
and phase task codes, 12
and project cost estimating, 41
Hourly billing, 50, 51
and job costing, 46
and project cost estimating, 40–41
Hybrid billing, 57

Indirect expenses, 181–83
Insurance, 188, 209–10
  liability, 199
  unemployment, 183, 198, 200
  workmen's compensation, 71–72, 184, 199
Interest expense, 208
Internal controls, 214–20
Internal Revenue Service. *See* Taxes
Investment costs, 184
Investment tax credit, 201
Invoices. *See* Billing

Job costing, 45–49
  and overhead rate, 36
  and phase task codes, 11, 13
  and time accounting, 24
Joint venture projects, 98–99

Labor, costs of, 29, 45–46, 173. *See also* Payroll; Time accounting
Letter of introduction, 130
Liability insurance, 183, 199
Limited partnerships, 99
Loans, 190, 191–92

Mailmerge, 128
Marketing
  advertising, 82, 89–90, 125–34
  A/E firm data base, 115–17
  attitudes, 81–88, 143–44
  budget for, 93–94, 134
  buttonholing, 79–80
  client data base, 91, 100, 104–15
  goals for, 94–95
  identifying clients, 90–91, 96–103, 144
  importance of, 79, 165–66
  intelligence, 118–24
  market analysis, 90–92
  news publication data base, 138
  public relations, 89, 93–94, 135–42
  referrals, 161–64
  selling, 92–93, 143–60
Matching FICA. *See* FICA tax
Moving average, 38, 39, 42, 48, 182

Newsletters, 131–32

Outside audit, 219–20
Overhead rate, 36–39, 92
  and direct vs. indirect expenses, 181–82
  and hourly billing, 51
  and job costing, 48
  and rental costs, 123–24
Overtime, 67–68
Owner draw, 33, 72–73, 201

Partnerships, 33, 72
Patrons, 86–87
Payables, 194. *See also* Accounts payable
Payroll, 63–73
  compensation time, 70–71
  costs of, 71–73, 196–202
  deductions, 66
  direct vs. indirect, 29, 33
  fixed vs. variable, 179–80
  frequency, 16, 17, 19, 61, 63–64
  general ledger distribution, 67–70
  IRS regulations, 63, 64–66, 68, 69–70
  overtime, 66–67
  owner draw, 33, 72–73, 201
  and phase task codes, 11–12. *See also* Time accounting

Percentage of construction cost billing, 54–56
Percentage of phase completed billing, 51–54
Personnel reports, 70
Phase task codes, 4–14
  and billing, 51–53
  format, 8–10
  phases, 5–7
  and project cost estimating, 42–44
  tasks, 7–8
  uses, 10–12
Presentation, 148–50
Price changes, 211
Print advertising, 133–34
Private sector clients, 96–97
Professional societies, 85
Project cost estimating, 40–44
  and job costing, 45
  limitations of formulas for, 157–59
  and phase task codes, 10–11. *See also* Bidding
Project number, 21–22
Project type, 20–21
Proof of cash, 217
Public records, 121–22
Public relations, 89, 93–94, 135–42
  brochures, 83–84, 135–36
  club membership, 84–85, 136
  print media, 137–40
  service organizations, 87, 137
  social gatherings, 83, 140–41
Public sector clients, 97–98
Purchase order system, 218–19

Qualification, 145–48
Questionnaires, 121, 131

Receivables, 192–93. *See also* Accounts receivable
Referrals, 114, 161–64
Reimbursables, 33, 48–49, 194–95
Rental costs, 123–24, 173

Self-employment tax, 72
Selling, 81–82, 92–93, 143–60
  closing, 153–55
  moving client off dead center, 154–56
  objections, 150–53
  presentation, 148–50
  qualification, 145–48
Service charges, 209
Service contracts, 212–13
Service costs, 211–12
Signature authority, 215, 216
Social security tax. *See* FICA tax
Sole proprietorship, 33, 72. *See also* Owner draw
Spread sheets, 40, 43–44
Square foot billing, 56–57
State unemployment insurance, 200
State unemployment tax, 198
Sub Chapter S Corporation, 72–73, 201

Taxes, 183–84
  and accounting methods, 58
  budgeting, 205
  and capital investment, 189
  federal withholding, 65, 68
  FICA, 65, 68, 71, 183, 196–97
  FUTA, 71, 183, 198–99
  payroll regulations, 63, 64–66, 68, 69–70, 71
  penalties, 64–65, 197–99, 210
  self-employment, 72
  state unemployment, 198
Telemarketing, 132–33
Telephone survey, 118–20
Temporary employment services, 200
Testimonial letters, 162

Time accounting, 15–25
  analysis, 24–25
  direct vs. indirect time, 6, 13, 23, 26, 67–68
  format, 19–24
  frequency, 15–19, 63
  and phase task codes, 10
  and project cost estimating, 41
  utilization rates, 26–28
  and work in progress, 62
Triplicate of choice, 147

Unbilled services, 62
Unearned income, 189
Unemployment insurance, 183–98, 200
Utilization rates, 26–28, 157–59

Variable expenses, 179–80, 205, 207
Variance. *See* Budget variance

Weekly time sheets, 16–17
Work in progress, 61–62
Workmen's compensation insurance, 71–72, 184, 199